REDISCO`
THE REFORMATION

REDISCOVERING
THE REFORMATION

LEARNING FROM THE ONE CHURCH
IN ITS STRUGGLES

MATTHEW KNELL

MONARCH
BOOKS

Published by
Lion Hudson Limited
Wilkinson House, Jordan Hill Business Park
Banbury Road, Oxford OX2 8DR, England
www.lionhudson.com

ISBN 978 0 8572 1905 3
e-ISBN 978 0 8572 1906 0

First edition 2019

Acknowledgments
Scripture quotations are primarily taken from the Holy Bible, New International Version Anglicized. Copyright © 1979, 1984, 2011 Biblica, formerly International Bible Society. Used by permission of Hodder & Stoughton Ltd, an Hachette UK company. All rights reserved. "NIV" is a registered trademark of Biblica. UK trademark number 1448790.

A catalogue record for this book is available from the British Library

Printed and bound in the UK, March 2019, LH26

*For mum and dad, who have shown me what it is to
have a living faith inspired by divine grace.*

CONTENTS

INTRODUCTION

Why do we need to rediscover the Reformation? Did we lose it somewhere? Surely all the celebrations of the 500th anniversary in 2017 indicate that the Reformation still has a significant influence on the church today. There seems no doubt that Protestant groups continue to think of the Reformation as the root from which they have all grown and which still gives some unity to the movement, despite all the obvious differences.

The origins of this book lie in a set of anniversary-year seminars delivered at Spring Harvest 2017 under the title "Rediscovering the Reformation", which looked at this landmark period in the history of the church. In preparing for these I began to realize that what the church was celebrating was as much a modern reconstruction of the Reformation as anything related to the events that took place. This was confirmed by the second source for this book, which was my research into reformation thought on the topics of sin, grace, and free will for another work that has just been published.[1] For that book, I read through the theological works of some of the major reformers – Luther, Zwingli, Calvin – as well as the Catholic reforming Council of Trent. As I came to appreciate the breadth of their own writings, freed from later selections

---

1   M. Knell, *Sin, Grace and Free Will: A Historical Survey of Christian Thought: Volume 2* (Cambridge: James Clarke, 2018) – shameless self-advertising.

and interpretations, I realized that common approaches to reformers' lives and thoughts in the anniversary celebrations and generic studies were far removed from the debates and work of the first half of the sixteenth century.

A prime example of this is what have become known as the five *solae* applied to the Reformation: faith alone, grace alone, Scripture alone, glory to God alone, Christ alone. Each of these, rightly understood, is a great truth of Christianity and a useful approach to the Christian faith. Whether and how they were used in the early sixteenth century, however, differed greatly from how I have heard them applied today.

"Faith alone" was certainly taught, by Martin Luther in particular, and the phrase itself was the most used of the five during the Reformation. Today, though, there seems to be confusion between this and "belief alone", as if faith and belief were synonymous, which they certainly were not in Luther's work. Faith is the core orientation of the whole of a person, whereas belief is primarily a rational engagement with God's revelation. Faith alone can also be confused with grace alone, another slogan used in the Reformation, yet grace is God's activity in salvation whereas faith is part of the divinely inspired human response. Grace also has huge dynamics in the reformers' writings because of their context as those integrated into the history of Christian thought, and thus sacramental grace plays an important role, as do the nature and role of the Spirit in grace, where too often we speak and sing of grace solely in relation to Christ.

"Scripture alone" is an interesting phrase that does reflect the reformers' desire to place the church back under the authority of the Bible, yet can be misunderstood to imply that "all we need is the Bible". As we will see, the Bible was still the preserve of the church and its correct interpretation was viewed as a key part of the work of the Holy Spirit. The idea of individual Christians reading as authorities on their own to discover meanings in Scripture was not the vision of the reformers. One of the most notable aspects of reading Luther, Calvin, et al. directly, rather than studies of the Reformation, is the number of quotations from church history that are used as part of their interpretation of Scripture and expression of the Christian faith. This was not a movement that simply started again with the Bible, but rather reflected a desire to return the church to what it should be.

It is rather strange to link "glory to God alone" (in Latin, *soli Deo Gloria*) with the Protestant reformers, since in the sixteenth century this term was used in far more Catholic documents than Protestant ones – though the reformers had nothing to say against the idea, of course, and did use it themselves. "Christ alone" is another phrase that is right when correctly applied, but which does carry dangers. Protestant reformers elevated Christ above the role of humans (and the saints) in salvation, against an emphasis on human-initiated work. This had been the subject of a lengthy debate within Catholicism, and there was certainly no unified approach to it in Catholic thought. The greatest voice in favour of the human role was Desiderius Erasmus, a philosopher who wanted to reform the church rather than the standard voice on this issue, and it was his work that Luther in particular wrote against in focusing on the work of God in Christ. But the Protestant reformers did not elevate Christ above Father and Spirit in salvation – perhaps "God alone" would be a better term, as the right roles of all three are necessary. This may guard against language such as "all I need for salvation is Christ", a concept that would have shocked reforming thinkers.

Therefore, while each of the *solae* is related to reforming thought, and some of them were used extensively by reformers, the emphasis placed on them in the sixteenth century is often not the one that accompanies their usage today. This does not necessarily mean that later applications are incorrect, but, if we want to understand the significance of the Reformation for the church in what it was at the time and what reformers were trying to do, we need to hold our current understanding lightly and be willing to recognize that the original Protestants may not have thought of the faith in the same way we do today. The goal of any such study for me is an enriching of my faith as it is challenged and expanded by learning from brothers and sisters from the past and those living in different contexts in the world today.

What stands out from the writings of the various reforming groups is that they were primarily desirous of reforming the church rather than rebooting it. The major thinkers were incredibly well schooled in church thought through the centuries and drew heavily on earlier writers who communicated a biblical faith well, as well as upholding the great creeds as examples of faith statements that reflected a scriptural understanding of God and his work in salvation. They feared what has been termed the "Radical Reformation" as being possibly worse than Catholicism in prioritizing humanity in the understanding and expression of Christian thought.

The result of this is that the context of their thought is not just the situation of the church in the early sixteenth century, or even in the late medieval period, when some of the corruptions in faith and practice began to be clearly evident in parts of the church. The proposed reforms were intended to help the church be what it should be, what at times it had been, and there was no desire to go back to a church that struggled with the person and nature of Christ or the concept of the Spirit, which was the situation as it emerged from New Testament times and in the first few centuries.

Here is the core of the problem that was present in the anniversary celebrations and in much thought about the Reformation: a lack of awareness of the full context of thought that was present in the discussions about faith and practice. There seems to be a rhetoric that holds that Protestantism comes from the reformers, and the reformers' ideas came from the Bible. Such a view does no justice to the projects that were undertaken to reform the church, and indeed such an approach to Scripture apart from tradition was rejected by the major figures.

There are theology degrees in which the only part of Christian history studied is the Reformation, and where the first sessions may look only at its immediate causes in the late medieval period. I do not know how any student is supposed to understand what Luther, Calvin, or any other major figure wrote without having a thorough grounding in the Church Fathers, particularly Augustine, or in the major figures of the early medieval period, primarily Lombard and Aquinas, since it is in the web of all this tradition that their thought develops and is defined. The result can only be a sense of rebooting the church, since too little is known of the church that existed in various forms through its history to discern what the reformers were aiming at.

Another aspect that does not often come across well in popular conceptions of the sixteenth century involves the divisions that were present between protesting groups, with the concept of "*the* Reformation" perhaps indicating too united a movement. To redress this, it will be necessary to look briefly at some of the clearer streams of reforming thought at this time, some of which sought to reform with a lower-case "r", while others wanted reform with a capital "R". The different movements sprang up largely independently, often at the same time in different parts of Europe. There is little that can be found to unite them, certainly in regard to their theology. In fact, the harshest statements of the time were often made by reformers about other reformers and reforming groups.

The dissension most commonly agreed on was over the authority of the pope, which only the Catholic reformers sought to uphold. Even the doctrine of transubstantiation (that in Communion, the bread and the wine actually become the body and the blood of Christ), while a major factor in creating some unity in opposition to this idea, did not lead to unity behind a single alternative understanding of the Lord's Supper. Rather, this was one area where the various reforming groups were most divided and even here there was an exception within Protestantism that for a time upheld the doctrine: the early stages of the reformed Church of England, which upheld transubstantiation in the Six Articles that were published in 1539.

Where the Protestant reformers joined together was in challenging the authority of the papacy and the church in matters of faith. By the beginning of the sixteenth century the papacy had a questionable enough history to allow people to speak out against the leader of the church in the West. This might not sound radical to modern ears, so ready are we to criticize our leaders, but it shows the massive movement that Western society had undergone in the later medieval period.

There are two important factors in this shift. The first concerns how people were tied into the church, with the bishop of Rome at its head. Since the fall of the Western Roman empire in the fifth century and the descent into the dark times of early medieval Europe with its small, fragile, agrarian states, the church had fulfilled two key roles: the guardianship of people's eternal destiny, which often dominated over earthly identity, with life expectancy generally short and few opportunities for social mobility; and the source of meaning, purpose, and knowledge, given that only churchmen were involved in considering these areas for many centuries. Together these meant that challenging the church on any topic was for a long time both difficult, in creating an opposing case, and dangerous, with the threat of excommunication that would consign a person to eternal damnation. The fact that people were able to break with Rome by the early sixteenth century shows that something had happened in society.

The source of meaning for people had changed from the church to society, in which the church was still an important voice, but now one of many. The major beginnings of this can be seen in the thirteenth century with the introduction to Western Europe of Aristotelian as well as Jewish and Arabian thought, which provided alternative authorities in many areas of life. Once the church's monopoly on knowledge and meaning was broken, the way was open for people to find truth, even religious truth, outside its boundaries. This does not mean that the church as a whole was the subject of attack, but that perceived errors in teaching and especially in morals were challenged, with an increasingly urban, educated, middle-class population unwilling to follow the church as readily as previous generations.

When attacks were made on the conduct in office of priests, monks, and even bishops, the implications were not critical for the nature and authority of the church, and there were reforming periods that bore such critiques in mind. Much more serious were attacks on the popes, because these undermined fundamental notions of Western Christianity, and we will pick up on this in later chapters. Sadly, by the early sixteenth century, the office of the bishop of Rome had become rather too easy to attack. This was partly owing to developments early in the medieval period, partly because of well-known incidents. This is the second factor that allowed for criticism of the church and the possibility of people "breaking" with the church.

We will explore the nature of the church in greater detail later on, but it is important at this stage to highlight this central concern about the papacy and its ability to exercise doctrinal authority that united all the reforming groups, except of course the reform that took place within the Catholic Church. There may not have been a single Reformation, but there was a common protest. An important point to note, however, is that this protest had a strong focus on authority and method rather than being purely about content or doctrine. Each of the reforming groups had issues with certain areas of Christian belief, but the protesting groups did not agree on the areas that they wanted to be corrected. The core faith expressed in the historic creeds was not challenged, although the communication of these, particularly as regards justification, was clearly a problem, as we will see later.

PURPOSE AND METHOD

So what will this book try to bring to the church's understanding as we "Rediscover the Reformation"? The first aim is to help any Christian to appreciate the developing ideas of the church in certain areas through its first 1,500 years, a period that Protestant churches tend rather to ignore, yet one containing much thought and practice that is rich, faithful, and beautiful. The second is to situate the thoughts of various relevant reforming voices in their rightful context to see what reforms were proposed and why, and how the different reformers viewed the need for reform. One point to make here is that I will try my utmost to present the teaching of different individuals and groups rather than just my own views or assessments.

Given the length of this book, one result of this approach is that a lot of history of thought is crammed into fewer words than one might like. It should therefore be viewed as a first stage for those really wanting to wrestle with the concepts being addressed, highlighting the thinkers and principles that we need to be aware of behind the ideas that the writers of the Reformation period were communicating. For those just wanting to dip their toes into Christian history, this book should help them understand that the Reformation was in fact a series of proposed reforms to the existing church rather than a brand new movement to reinvent Christianity from starting principles.

An additional motivation behind the book comes from the Spring Harvest theme of 2017, which sought unity in the church. If there is only one church, as Christ had only one body, then what we are studying in the history of Christian thought and practice are the ideas and lives of our brothers and sisters from different contexts with different thought patterns and different strengths and weaknesses. While the church has been all too keen to find weaknesses in others and to condemn them, surely it is preferable to admit that none of us has everything sorted and understood, and thus to listen humbly to each other to seek understanding, recognizing that this will not necessarily mean agreement on all issues, in order to enrich our understanding of our God, our faith, and the lives we are called to live.

The book has been arranged by theme, with four major studies and one additional area that will be considered. The four core themes are the nature of the church, the approach to Scripture, grace as the divine agent in salvation, and then faith, belief, and works as the human response to salvation. In each of these, the relevant history of the church will be outlined before we look at various proposed reforms from different groups and individuals in the sixteenth century. The final study looks at persecution, again noting its roots in the history of the church before considering two accounts from the English church at the time of the Reformation. The focus in the Reformation period is on the first stages, roughly up until 1560, rather than on later developments as the early movements began to bed in in different contexts.

One result of this approach is that the various protesting voices can be differentiated from each other, which I hope will weaken the idea of a single Reformation that would pit the Protestants against the Catholics. The fact is that there were significant differences *between* reforming groups, most obviously between the best-known reformers and the radical reformers. As well as these differences within the protests of the sixteenth century, this book also highlights some major departures from early Protestant thought in churches today that come under the umbrella of modern Protestantism. The clearest example of this would be the major reformers' strong support for infant baptism, when there are many Protestant churches today that do not continue that practice.

The decision to approach each of the studies through the history of thought will mean that there is some repetition of historical factors in different chapters. All being well, this will not be too frustrating for the reader, as it is necessary if we are going to examine the precise role of these factors in each instance. It is also hoped that the repetition will reinforce both knowledge and understanding of key stages of the church's development.

Before we move on to the major themes, it seems sensible to do a brief survey of the major individuals and groups that were proposing reforms during the first forty to fifty years after Luther composed the 95 Theses. This will help the reader to understand the character of the precise voice that will then speak into the various aspects of Christian faith and practice that will be presented through the history of the church and into the reforming period.

THE REFORMATIONS

While there may not have been a single, united "Reformation", there were a number of reformations active in the first half of the sixteenth century that we need to survey before we look at their relationship to church and Scripture. Scholars of the Reformation period will each have their own opinion on how many groups they would identify and on what basis. I see five major reformations and one important but disconnected movement, which will now be introduced in historical order. The purpose of this is to emphasize aspects that will be elaborated on in later chapters rather than seeking to cover all the aspects of each reformation.

Luther

Where else could we start? The publication of Martin Luther's 95 Theses (probably not nailed to the doors of Wittenberg Church, although that makes a better story) was the event that marked the beginning of the sixteenth-century reformations. We will leave the discussion of these, indulgences, faith, and grace to the relevant chapter later in the book and concentrate here on the wider nature of Luther's reforms. One of the first things that readers new to Luther's writings generally comment on is how Catholic he sounds, and for one very good reason: he *was* very Catholic in most of his thought. Luther was inspired by his reading of the apostle Paul and Augustine of Hippo, the father of Catholic theology, and in many of the points that he raised against the church of his time Luther was calling the Catholic Church back to its roots. Again, we must always bear in mind that most of the dissenting voices in the early sixteenth century were for a reform, not a restart, of the church.

The more I study it, the more Luther's Reformation fascinates me. I had imbibed a notion that Luther stood on one side and the Catholic Church on the other, and that the resulting split was therefore inevitable. There are many errors in this idea. Luther gradually developed ideas that disagreed with the church of his time, initially seeking reform from within the church through disputation. Even as late as 1541 there was a major initiative to bring the two sides together at Regensburg.

Luther's reforms were comparatively limited in their extent, but were focused on core areas of the faith, and there was little in his theology that was not already present in some Catholic thinkers and writers. He was against those additions and extensions to theology that had greatly affected the believer's approach to God through Christ and Spirit. The purpose of translating the Bible and making the faith more accessible was not to bring down the church but to purify it. Initially, Luther believed that this could be done under papal authority, although this soon changed and he realized that the church he was looking for required a change in the nature of its leadership.

While Luther did take on the Catholic Church where he perceived errors in its method and theology, he applied the same vigour to critiquing other reforming thinkers whom he saw as equally dangerous to the people of Europe. Luther's own Reformation in Wittenberg was taken over by Andreas von Karlstadt, who gradually departed from many of Luther's teachings and ended up being expelled on Luther's orders. There were other more extreme views being expressed that incurred Luther's great written wrath. Luther fell out with Zwingli over the matter of the Lord's Supper, with the former condemning again not only the theology that was taught but – more importantly – the method of reading Scripture that was used as the basis for that theology.

As a result, there is a certain chaos to a study of Luther's Reformation in respect of its development and relationship with other individuals and groups. Luther's views on a number of matters change, and as a result his critiques of others change. The safety net behind all this was the political support that Luther received from Elector Frederick, who hid him away in the castle at Wartburg for a couple of years to protect him from opposition – this proved to be a vital time early in the Reformation for Luther to work on his writing, including his translation of the New Testament.

It is therefore very difficult to nail down Luther's Reformation and say that it was this or that. The extent of his written output is quite extraordinary and the set entitled *Luther's Works* is still seeing new volumes published, having reached number 88. He wrote biblical commentaries, sermons, theological works, articles for disputation, works on political theology. For those who love a bit of chaos Luther is a great subject for study, but throughout all his work one sees a passion for God and the gospel whether or not one agrees with his content or his style at every point.

Ulrich Zwingli

Zwingli has a very different approach to reforming the church from that of Martin Luther. Where Luther moves slowly through various realizations that the church of which he is a part has faults, Zwingli is critical earlier in his life and ministry, as his humanist education and the more independent Swiss context free him from some of the constraints that Luther only slowly breaks out of. In particular, Zwingli asserts the authority of the Bible above the traditional interpretations early in his preaching career, something for which he is notable, and the result is a more radical reform proposed from the beginning of the changes in Zurich.

Zwingli's reform was consistent in its message and approach, focusing on the authority of Scripture and the sovereignty of God. The challenge from the Catholic Church was not great in Zurich – the council of the city had appointed Zwingli to high ecclesial office knowing his different approach to Scripture and tradition, and the reforming agenda gradually led to a separation from the authority of Rome – and although there was some division created by Anabaptist groups, Zwingli's victories over these in debate created a clear leadership and direction for the reformation in the city.

That there was no significant spread of Zwingli's Reformation across Europe may firstly be accounted for by other more prominent factions voicing the protest: the more obvious appeal of Luther as the flag-bearer of Protestantism, the radical reformers' spirituality, and later Calvin's great theological/ecclesial/social project that drew in Protestants from around Europe. Secondly, Zwingli's own demise must be considered a factor, as he fell in a military engagement with invading Catholic forces. With the loss of its figurehead, the reformation that had been accomplished in Zurich continued along its own path, allowed to do so by the Catholic powers, but, compared with other groups, it lacked the power to spread its message.

The Radical Reformation

This is not a term used in the sixteenth century, but it has become a standard designation for a range of protesting groups, particularly in the early decades of the Reformation, that sought a clearer split between the state and the church than was advocated by Luther, Zwingli, or Calvin. At the time, the most common word used to describe these was "Anabaptist", since rebaptism (the meaning of the word) was a common teaching against the sacraments of the Catholic Church, but this would not cover all of the groups who were considered radical. Other terms such as "fanatics" and "spiritualists" were also applied, both by Catholics and by other major reformers.

Today the first person associated with Anabaptism in the early years of the Reformation is Menno Simons, and worthily so. We have more of Simons' writings than of any other early leaders, and his legacy is clearer to see in the groups that developed and continue, some bearing his name. Simons was certainly on the extreme moderate wing of the Anabaptist movement, but does not seem to have made a great impact on other reformers, who focused on other parts of the movement. Simons worked primarily in Holland and north Germany, being persecuted by political powers on several occasions for the disruption to religion that he and the Anabaptist groups brought, and he spent much of his time helping Anabaptists develop a true, biblical faith and appropriate Christian lives and worship.

While Simons has had the most solid and lasting impact, he was not the first to spring to most people's minds when they thought about radical reforming groups in the early decades of the Reformation, and his Anabaptist beliefs would have meant that many would have grouped him with the more widely influential people associated with the movement. The first of these groups to be mentioned are the Zwickau prophets, a group from just south of Wittenberg who taught the absolute authority of the Spirit above and even apart from Christ and the church. Some members of this group came to Wittenberg and were sent away (as they had been from Zwickau), but their presence brought this form of Anabaptism to the forefront of the awareness of reforming groups. One individual greatly influenced by the Zwickau prophets was Thomas Müntzer, who continued to spread a similar message as he travelled across Europe.

A second important early voice was that of Andreas von Karlstadt, who had mentored Luther and then been led to a Protestant faith by Luther himself. While Luther was secreted in the Wartburg, Karlstadt took on the leadership of the reformation in Wittenberg, but his views on images and the Lord's Supper (and later on baptism and church reform) led to Luther returning and sending Karlstadt into exile. For Luther, Karlstadt's great sin was not recognizing the authority of the Bible in matters of faith, but being willing to change the meaning of Scripture to fit with his theology and spirituality.

There were Anabaptists in Zurich who challenged Zwingli's reform on the basis that Zwingli's recognition of the Bible as the sole authority should mean that he would reject infant baptism, as there is no explicit mention of this in Scripture. Zwingli took them to task in a similar manner to Luther, arguing that the practice was strongly implied in Scripture and was the accepted practice of the church from its beginning, and thus the Anabaptists were, in his opinion, placing their own views above Scripture and the church.

The most notable event in the public perception of the radical reformers occurred in Münster in the mid-1530s, when the city was taken over by visionary leaders who claimed their revelations had authority over everything else. On this basis they infamously legalized polygamy and instituted a kind of communist monarchical city-state that attracted many from around Europe who were seeking a heightened spiritual experience, including a number from the churches being guided by Menno Simons.

In Geneva, Calvin was in correspondence with a radical thinker named Michael Servetus. While Servetus denied infant baptism, and therefore could be deemed an "Anabaptist", his most notorious work was one that denied the Trinity, and it was this that was central to his being put on trial for heresy, with Calvin as his accuser. The sentence of death was no surprise, given the outrage extending far beyond Geneva at his views (the death sentence for heresy shows the severity with which faith issues were considered), and although Calvin asked for Servetus to be beheaded rather than burned (as a lesser punishment), Servetus was burned to death. The incident has been used by some to accuse Calvin of unacceptable severity, but such a view shows no awareness of the culture of the time and Calvin's role in the affair comes across more as that of a defender of the faith and a moderate voice compared to others involved.

This catalogue of radical reforming groups and figures dominated the perception of the Anabaptist/fanatic movement that arose alongside the more rational protesting voices. The severest critiques of such groups came not from the Catholic Church, which viewed them as an inevitable result of removing control of the faith from the established church, but from major reformers who feared that their movements would be tainted by being grouped together with these "Protestants" or that they would lose followers – as they did – who wished for the heightened experience offered rather than obedience to God and his word.

John Calvin

John Calvin formed his Protestant thought while still in his native France, and with his analytical mind recognized that he was not a papist and decided to consider the teachings of the various reforming groups in developing his own theology. He travelled around several early Protestant lands, ending up staying in Geneva only because of a rather bizarre incident in which the leader of reform in that city, Guillaume Farel, cursed Calvin's future life and career if he did not stay to implement reform. Calvin gave sufficient credence to these curses to stay and, apart from one period of exile after a disagreement with the city council, remained there until the end of his life.

Calvin's reformation is often associated with what is known as the Geneva Experiment, a lived-out version of some of his core theology. But the reform that Calvin instituted was both broader and deeper than that embodied in Geneva, and is best encapsulated in the developing *Institutes of the Christian Religion* that was first published in 1536 and then revised multiple times over the next twenty years.

With a basis in this extensive, systematic theology, Calvin's reformation is the most stable of those we have looked at so far, and based on a concept of Scripture as God-breathed both in its composition and then in its interpretation. For those coming to it for the first time, Calvin's work is notable for the extensive use of historical voices to clarify his teaching, generally in support of his positions although sometimes as warnings about errors that can creep in when human reason plays too strong a role.

The strength of Calvin's reformation was its coherence regarding Christian faith and life, and we must recognize that there were many other important thinkers who were associated with this reformation yet were distinct and powerful in their own right, from some of whom Calvin learned aspects of his thought – Martin Bucer in Strasbourg is one example. Calvin did not lead the Reformation in the sense of being the arbitrator of any disputes, but Geneva did provide a home for people with similar views who had fled persecution, and the *Institutes* was the most clearly worked-through theological treatise.

Calvin wrote extensively beyond the *Institutes*, in commentaries on books of the Bible and in theological battles with opponents. What is perhaps most surprising when reading Calvin from this distance is the gap between much of his theology and that of groups that today are associated with the great reformer. One thinks first of his engagement with the tradition of the church and his views on infant baptism in this regard, but beyond this Calvin's deep ideas on the Holy Spirit and his nuanced understanding of God's sovereignty also do not always come across well in modern movements. Given the richness of Calvin's writing, it is a shame that so often rather simplified parodies seem to be all that people know.[2]

Anglicanism

We need to start with Henry VIII and his wives simply because this is the first thought that jumps into most people's minds

---

[2]   This would also apply to Luther, although in the Lutheran tradition there is a clearer progression of thought from the root, whereas with Calvin it is often modern movements that spring up and claim a link by using the term "Calvinist".

when they consider the Reformation in England. Certainly this was a factor, and it provided a trigger for the Act of Supremacy (1534) by which Henry became head of the church in England. Henry famously desired a son (and Anne Boleyn), and sought to annul his marriage to Catherine of Aragon to further these desires on the basis that the marriage was illegitimate. That much is familiar to everyone. What may be less familiar is the wider background to the reformation in England both in the medieval period and within Henry's own lifetime.

If there were one country ripe for reformation in the early sixteenth century, it was England. English society had always been less respectful of authority than mainland Europe, as shown by events like the Magna Carta, and this spilled quickly into the religious sphere with works like *Piers Plowman* (a harshly sarcastic critique of the church and its leaders) and Wycliffe's call for the authority of the Bible, and indeed the translation of the Bible that he inspired. The idea of freedom from papal authority was thus not as radical in the English context as elsewhere in Europe.

The English Reformation, when it happened, was a rather curious beast in the early years. Henry himself had famously been granted the title "Defender of the Faith" for his writing against Martin Luther in the early 1520s. He had then appealed to Luther for support in his project to be rid of Catherine of Aragon and had received no encouragement. The man who did help, Archbishop Thomas Cranmer, had travelled in Europe and met various reforming groups, being apparently most impressed by those loosely associated with Calvin's project, given the number of these men who were invited over to teach in Cambridge in the late 1530s.

While Cranmer was vital in securing Henry's divorce, this did not give him the leadership of the Reformation that developed from the Act of Supremacy, even as Archbishop of Canterbury. The leader was very clearly Henry, an astute theologian who composed many of the key early documents of the Reformation in England. The project in the 1530s and 1540s was an interesting one, given that it was not driven by great theological revelations or particular problems with the existing church (except the pope's intransigence over Catherine). There was thus no need to reform except where the leaders perceived faults, and no single basis on which to reform, with strong Catholic, Lutheran, and reformed voices all present.

The clearest example of this tentative approach can be found in the Six Articles of 1539, which continued to support the doctrine of transubstantiation, the one doctrine that all other protesting groups were united in rejecting. The task of reforming the church must also be considered in the light of a wider political factor, which was the stability of the Tudor dynasty and the strength of England in relations with other countries. Both of these were at the top of Henry's overall priorities for his reign, as he was only the second in a new dynasty that had emerged to bring an end to the chaos that had resulted from the Wars of the Roses.

In order to create this stability, Henry needed one major thing from his new religion: that it unite the country in the spiritual sphere to protect it from fragmentation from these sources. This was a common fear of rulers across Europe for the next century at least, and much of the suffering of Christians of different denominations resulted from the desire of rulers to provide unity of faith as a basis for a unity of identity and then action. This principle was vital to the end of the religious wars between Catholics and Lutherans that was accomplished by the Peace of Augsburg in 1555, which included the thought *cuius regio, eius religio* ("whose kingdom, their religion"), with wider effects for other Protestant groups agreed at the Peace of Westphalia in 1648.

The reformation of the church in England thus needed to be a unifying force, and one can see, not only in Henry's reforms but also in the church as it developed under Cranmer after Henry's death, a breadth or perhaps flexibility to the wording that seeks to allow different approaches to reform to participate. Catholics who continued to uphold papal authority were naturally excluded, but beyond this there was little to disbar Catholics from the new church, while people influenced by other reforming groups were likewise welcome. There would be a similar situation after the restoration of Anglicanism under Elizabeth I, when her "settlement" sought to appease both Catholic and reforming groups, often to the satisfaction of neither party.

Catholic Reformation

This is an important part of the reforming movements in the first fifty years of the Reformation and a major step in the history of the Catholic Church. It was not the first attempt at reform; most notably there had been widespread reforms initiated with some success in the early fifteenth century during a period known as the "Conciliar Papacy", when councils had gained greater authority and individual popes were slightly less significant in Catholic faith and practice.

Many voices were calling for reform of the church by the early sixteenth century, some of which ultimately rejected the church under Rome and formed Protestant movements, some of which stayed under the authority of Rome and sought to reform the church from within. Desiderius Erasmus and Martin Luther fell out over whether reform was possible within the church, with Erasmus continuing to believe it was. As regards the major teachings of the Protestant reformers – certainly Luther, Zwingli, Calvin, and Cranmer – there was nothing that was new to the Catholic Church, nothing that had not been taught at some point and recognized as true, and little that was not being taught somewhere within the Catholic Church even during the sixteenth century.

It is always slightly dubious to talk about "a" Catholic Church, as it varies greatly in faith and practice in its papal, scholastic, mystical, monastic (of various forms), popular, and political manifestations, as well as through its historical developments both positive and more controversial. In many ways this is the shame of the Council of Trent (1545–63), which clarified the Catholic position in the light of protesting thought: it defined Catholic theology as much as reformed it, and thus to some extent limited the development of Catholic thought in the succeeding period.

My problem is not that Tridentine theology (as that coming out of the Council of Trent is known) is not in line with previous Catholic thought, but that it certainly does not encompass all the richness of this history, while certain aspects are clearly written to oppose Protestant ideas and thus feel more reactive than constructive. There are some beautiful elements, but also clear lines drawn separating Catholics from Protestants and creating sharp divisions in the church that have only recently begun to close, most notably after Vatican II (1962–5), which acknowledged a common faith professed by all Christian denominations despite disagreements over some teachings.

Having said all this, there were major reforms enacted at the Council of Trent, as a simple glance through the documents shows. For most of the sessions that discussed theology and the church, the doctrinal pronouncements are relatively brief, and generally much longer are the reforming statements that come in the second half, seeking to root out immorality in the church, to improve the education of both priests and laity, and to remove corruption in the appointment of people to various offices.

TIME TO BEGIN

The first fifty years of what has become known as "the Reformation" were thus quite complex when it comes to both relations between different groups and the nature of the reforms being proposed. It is of vital importance to recognize that this period cannot be separated out from the rest of church history into some kind of model of Bible-Reformation-Modern Church, or even Bible-Augustine-Reformation-Modern Church, as some would develop the idea, but that the reformations bore in mind all that had gone before, seeking purity of faith, teaching, and life both through the history and in their own context.

I trust that this is sufficient preparation for the first of the main studies that look at aspects of Christianity in various stages of development to allow a better understanding of different reforming perspectives in the early sixteenth century.

CHAPTER ONE

UNDERSTANDING THE CHURCH

One of the big decisions required when putting this book together was the order in which Scripture and church should be considered. The choice to put church first will seem strange to some readers, so it needs to be explained. This is not an issue of authority, as we will see that Scripture maintains the primary position. Rather, it is about history and method, recognizing both that there was a church before there was a Bible (the Old Testament Scriptures were obviously gathered earlier and will be considered in the next chapter), and that the church selects the books that will form the New Testament and guards the faith of believers not only in this selection but also in establishing teachings in line with those received from Christ and the apostles. Sometimes churches' teachings seem almost to imply that Christ ascended and left behind the New Testament, rather than sending his Spirit to inspire and form his body, the church, of which the writers and writings of New Testament documents were a part.

The nature and role of the church were a vital part of the discussions around the time of the Reformation. The major reformers were just that – reformers – who sought to bring the church back to its core teachings and duties and away from corruptions that had infected it, and this would also be true of the majority of the content in documents from the Catholic reforming Council of Trent. In considering this, we should avoid getting caught up in ideas of getting back to the church of New Testament times, or the earliest church, precisely because of the lack of authoritative scriptures and accepted doctrines at that point when these are so important in later disputes.

This chapter aims to trace some of the most important developments in thought on the church from the late first century through to the time of the Reformation, in order to illuminate the teachings of the reformers when they write about the church.

THE EARLY CHURCH

It's quite a challenge to provide a concise picture of the early church as a preparation for later reforming thought! It won't be necessary to look at every area of early church thought and life, but only to draw out relevant threads on the formation of the church with regard to both problems that would arise and strengths to which the reformers looked back. The New Testament writings generally refer to the church through images – body, bride, vine, building (not the physical building, but that of which Christ is the capstone) – rather than developing a systematic theology of the church, which has always made constructing a definitive concept of church difficult.

One important characteristic of the early church was the authority of the message that was being taught in the churches. This was particularly an issue because of the uncertainty about aspects of church teaching and perceived threats to the gospel that we will look at shortly. The perceived value of the church's message is evident already in the New Testament writings, with Paul encouraging Timothy to "[g]uard the good deposit that was entrusted to you" (2 Timothy 1:14), an encouragement that ends with the phrase "with the help of the Holy Spirit who lives in *us*". The plural pronoun "us" is interesting here, indicating a collective responsibility for protecting the message. Later in the same letter, the dangers that would face the church are also stated: "For the time will come when people will not put up with sound doctrine. Instead, to suit their own desires, they will gather around them a great number of teachers to say what their itching ears want to hear" (2 Timothy 4:3).

The evidence of the earliest Christian writings after the New Testament is both that the warning was just and that the church followed Paul's encouragement to remain true to the message they had received, despite the temptation to follow more attractive teachings. Bishop Polycarp of Smyrna, who was himself taught by the apostle John, echoes Paul's words to Timothy closely in his letter to the church at Philippi at the beginning of the second century:

> *Whoever does not confess that Jesus Christ has come in the flesh is antichrist; whoever does not confess the witness of the cross is of the devil; and whoever corrupts the oracles of the Lord to support their own desires, saying that there is neither resurrection nor judgment, that person is the firstborn of Satan. Therefore let us leave the empty actions of many along with their false teachings, and rather turn to the word that was delivered to us from the beginning, being sober in prayer and*

> *constant in fasting, praying to the all-seeing God*
> *with supplications that he will not lead us into*
> *temptation, just as the Lord said, "The Spirit is*
> *willing, but the flesh is weak".*

(Polycarp, *Letter to the Philippians*, 7:1–2)

Around the same time, Bishop Ignatius of Antioch writes on similar lines in his letters, warning the church to guard itself against "mad dogs" that stealthily bite at the truth. Ignatius praises the church at Ephesus for the way it resisted such false teachers:

> *I have learned that certain persons passed through*
> *you on their travels, bringing evil doctrine with*
> *them, but you did not allow them to sow their seed*
> *in you because you stopped your ears so that you*
> *would not receive the seed they had sown. You are*
> *stones of a temple that were prepared beforehand to*
> *be a building of God the Father, being hoisted up to*
> *the heights through the work of Jesus Christ, which is*
> *the cross, and using the Holy Spirit for a rope; your*
> *faith is your winch, and love is the way that leads up*
> *to God.*

(Ignatius, *Letter to the Ephesians*, 9:1)

In seeking to hold fast to the faith of the church, Christians are encouraged in this early period to submit themselves to the teachings of their leaders as the church in Acts listened to the apostles. An early bishop of Rome, Clement, writes on these lines to the church at Corinth:

> *Therefore it is right for us to learn from so great*
> *and so many examples, submit our necks and*
> *occupy a place of obedience, taking sides with those*
> *who are the leaders of our souls, so that in ceasing*
> *this foolish dissension we may gain the goal that*
> *lies before us in truthfulness, keeping away from*
> *every fault.*

(1 Clement 61:1)

A similar line on respect is shown in the *Didache,* or the *Teachings of the Twelve*, which discusses the appointment of leadership in a church:

> *Appoint for yourselves therefore bishops and*
> *deacons who are worthy of the Lord, men who are*
> *meek and not lovers of money, who are true and*
> *approved. They also perform a service for you of*
> *prophets and teachers. Therefore do not despise*
> *them for they are your honourable men along with*
> *the prophets and teachers.*

(*Didache,* 15:1–4)

Some of these key early Christian writings suggest that there were wandering Christian teachers who would be paid to preach in churches and who were popular because of the message they gave – often more pleasant than the encouragement to be united and persevere when suffering that the local leaders gave. There are repeated warnings against the division such teachers could create and a belief that churches should give first authority to the leaders that God has given them.

One important aspect of the early church is thus a sense of being a united body of faith across the Roman empire, something that was challenged both by the rapid spread of Christianity from the Near East across the empire and by the difficulty of some of the key points of the faith. By the end of the first century the apostles had all died, and there were questions about the faith that needed an authoritative witness to the truth. This is clearly provided by certain leaders who had learned the faith from the apostles and then by their successors – we have already had quotations from Clement, who early tradition claimed was taught by Peter, and from Polycarp and Ignatius, who were taught by John. These three had such a recognized authority that they were able to write to advise churches on matters of faith and practice, Clement writing a letter to Corinth, Polycarp to Philippi, and Ignatius to the Ephesians, the Magnesians, the Trallians, the Romans, the Philadelphians, and the Smyrnaeans.

Why is authority such an issue for the early church? Largely because of the difficulty of not only protecting the Christian message but even understanding it in the context of the first couple of centuries. What become the New Testament writings have a strongly Jewish focus because the majority are written when Jerusalem retains a central place in Christianity, before its destruction by the Romans in AD 70. However, the growing church around the empire is primarily Gentile and heavily influenced by Greek thought, which creates new problems for the church in understanding core elements of the Christian gospel.

One element that sums up the church's struggle is incarnation, which is clearly absolutely central to the gospel. There were two aspects of Greek thought that made it difficult for many to conceive that the eternal Word of God could take on flesh. First, there was the teaching on creation, concerning which many strains of Greek theological thinking sought to distance the perfect God (or Good) from the material world because of the corruption and imperfection evidenced in that world. Second, there was the nature of God, who was believed to be "impassible", incapable of change or suffering, which is problematic for an eternal Word that not only takes on flesh but even dies on a cross.

The challenges posed by just this one part of the surrounding cultural and philosophical influences on the early church demanded not only great devotion to the teaching of the gospel, but also an assurance that the message being taught in the church was that received from Christ and the apostles. Even for those churches with access to some or many of the writings that would form the New Testament, there are no simple replies to many of the perceived false teachings because, as we will see, there is little if any systematic theology in those stories and letters. As regards the incarnation, there is the added problem that the central term used to describe Jesus Christ, "the Son of God", can just as easily be considered in line with the Greek cultural understanding of God and the world as with the far more complex God-man of the Apostolic Tradition.

With a large number of oral and written sources beginning to circulate, some of uncertain origin, it is the church and its recognized leaders that quickly become the guardians of the faith as they affirm the core beliefs and begin to battle against those who have departed from sound teaching. A good early example of erroneous teaching would be Marcion of Sinope, a Gnostic teacher and the son of a bishop, who was confronted by Polycarp and declared "the firstborn of Satan" because of his departure from the faith of the church in denying the incarnation and the validity of the Jewish scriptures.

Through the first 300 years of Christianity, the Christians lived through persecutions and the pressures of pagan Roman society, having to deal with leaders and gatherings that denied important beliefs of the early church, with few writings recognized as an authority that could be used to test suspect teachings. The nature of Jesus Christ was the greatest issue that was faced, with recurrent voices emphasizing either his divinity or his humanity and the church bravely battling to assert both as coexisting in the one person.

One controversy that summed up many struggles of the early church, however, related to the Holy Spirit and the Spirit's relationship to the believer, to the church, and to the writings that the church was increasingly relying on through the second century. It concerned a prophet called Montanus and two prophetesses, Priscilla and Maximilla. The major issues that arose with this movement in Phrygia, modern-day Turkey, concerned not salvation but the teaching about the Spirit and the relationship between the Spirit, the church, and the developing Scriptures. The experience of the Spirit manifesting in prophecies and miracles was not new to the church – the gifts of the Spirit had always been affirmed and evidenced, and would continue to be for centuries to come. Montanus gained a significant following because of his holy life, his visions, and the miracles associated with his ministry, but his claim that he was the Father speaking in human form, and the claim to be the embodiment of the Paraclete (more associated with Maximilla) and thus to be uttering the very words of God, were rejected by the church. Such teachings did not totally depart from writings that would be included in the New Testament – Montanus sought to ground his teachings in passages from John's Gospel in particular – but they were against the faith that had been handed down and thus had to represent misinterpretations, such as the distinction between the Holy Spirit and the Paraclete.

Such ideas challenged the core notions of the Apostolic Tradition regarding the nature and purpose of the church, namely that, following Christ's ascension, the Spirit had been sent to form the church and guide it to hold true to the gospel that was transmitted through the apostles. If a lone voice, or group of voices, arose with a new divine authority above that of the church or the Christian writings, which could reject or reinterpret elements of the gospel message, then the assurance of believers and the unity of the body of Christ could not be maintained.

There are other aspects of the earliest church that could be explored – persecution, an emphasis on holiness, evangelism – but these were not the key points that arose during the Reformation discussions on the church. More central were questions of the faith that resided in the church and the transmission of that faith by the leaders. For the earliest church, these were vitally important because the New Testament books were as yet undecided and the faith was under threat from cultural and philosophical alterations, many of which came from Christians wrestling with the revelation of Christ in the context of their understanding of reality.

THE ESTABLISHMENT OF THE CHURCH

The Theological Project

Things change greatly for the church from the late third century, often gradually in some of the areas we are focusing on here.

One of these is the study and explanation of the Christian faith that began to develop at that time and reached early heights in discussions of the godhead in the fourth century, most notably in the great Councils at Nicaea (325) and Constantinople (381).

The earlier church seems to have loved its teachings and ideas, but was not overly theological or systematic in how it discussed and presented them. Partly this is because the church struggled to understand its beliefs well. The evidence of Celsus, a second-century Greek philosopher, is that the church was not a sophisticated entity during his life, being comprised largely of the disenfranchised – the poor, slaves, women – rather than the well-to-do and educated classes. Given that the work of creating more formal "Christian theology" requires a knowledge of philosophy for the precise use of words and concepts, there were few in the church who were able to take on such a project, particularly given the lack of contemporaries with whom they could safely discuss ideas or any schools that passed on formed Christian teaching. This situation makes the contribution of the few great early theologians, most notably Irenaeus of Lyon, all the more remarkable.

One key factor that complicated the subject of Christian belief was that there were many important areas of Christian thought that were strongly upheld but not clearly understood, particularly relating to the key figure of Jesus. The church knew that Jesus was a man, but also believed him to be divine. They knew that Jesus was not the Father, being the Son, but that Jesus' relationship with the Father was not that of any other human being. But the language of "Son of God" could easily end up separating Jesus from any notions of divinity, while emphasizing the unity of the Son with the Father could separate him from any real humanity. The church today talks easily about Jesus being fully God and fully man, often I think without properly appreciating what either of these phrases means or what the challenges are in asserting that Christ is in reality both.

There is great complexity in these ideas right at the heart of the Christian gospel without clear answers to all the surrounding questions. For the early church, the problem raised was less great than one might think, primarily because of the experience of God and a humility towards the teaching of the church and its leadership. That Christ was born of a virgin, lived, died, rose, and ascended, sending the Spirit to enliven and equip the church, was a matter of faith, not requiring an understanding of the metaphysical implications of any one part. In accepting this and experiencing the power of the Spirit individually and communally, the church was able to cling to the gospel through tough circumstances.

The need to develop a theological understanding of these and other ideas came not from the very nature and experience of the church itself, but from those – often Christians inside the church – who explored the teaching of the church and arranged it in ways that did not marry up with the standard presentation of the Christian message. Probably the most notable, and certainly a useful, example of this would be a man called Arius, a priest in the region of Alexandria in Egypt in the late third and early fourth centuries. Arius is now known as one of the great heretics of the church, but it is difficult to see this as his own purpose in exploring the Christian faith. He struggled with the teaching about Christ, particularly the fact that Jesus was the Son of God and yet was also spoken of as somehow God himself. Surely the language of "Son of God" indicated a particular relationship of origin – that the Son came from the Father – and therefore not only must the Son be less than the Father but also there must have been a point at which he was born of the Father? Clearly this must have taken place before the creation of this universe for the Word to be "with God in the beginning" (John 1:2), but the language did not seem to Arius to allow Christ to be raised up to the level of the Father, as the church generally taught.

We can see in this that Arius, like most who would be declared heretics, was working with elements of the Bible's teaching and seeking to honour this in challenging how the church had interpreted certain concepts. It was teachers such as Arius who were vital to the church's efforts to formalize an understanding of Christian thought in doctrinal statements, and primarily in the formation of creeds or statements of belief such as those produced by the Councils of Nicaea and Constantinople. The beliefs that were expressed through this period have been crucial ever since in the interpretation of Scripture for the church, the doctrines (when understood) acting as safeguards against false teachings.

The eventual result of this transition towards a stronger understanding of the Christian faith should ideally be an experience of salvation and the presence of the Spirit in the church, backed up by an assurance that this was in line with a deep understanding of the faith that could be passed down. Practically, for the church that emerged – and indeed still for the church of today – a split often grew between the experience and understanding of the individual believer and the theology of the church. Experience both personal and in a church context has often been too much moulded by cultural misunderstandings and has left behind the core teaching of the universal church, while theology can become a theoretical project in itself that can fail either to guide the church or to stay faithful to its origins. This split between error-strewn practice and overly philosophical theology would provide two important roots for reforming thought.

The Nature of the Western Church

A second important development was a change in the nature of the church in Western Europe, in its place in the overall church, in its internal structure, and in its relationship with secular society. The early centre of Christianity was clearly the eastern half of the Roman empire, and the language and thought system that dominated Christianity was Greek. Not only was the developing New Testament written in Greek, but the writings that communicated the Apostolic Tradition were also Greek, with only minor exceptions. By the time "schools" of Christian thought had developed (not educational institutions but common approaches to Christian thinking) in the fourth century, the two most notable were based in the East – at Alexandria and Antioch.

There were five (initially four) key centres of Christianity where the leaders of the churches were termed "Patriarchs": Jerusalem, Antioch, Alexandria, Rome, and Constantinople. These leaders were important in overseeing any doctrinal or pastoral matters that affected their churches, but they were not authorities in themselves, independent of the wider church. This is most clearly reflected in the great Councils of the church, where every member had an equal right to vote when discussing the most foundational beliefs. Supporting the Greek nature of the early church, these Councils were held in the East and produced statements of belief in Greek.

The two major halves of the Roman empire eventually each had their own capital, Rome and Constantinople, and their own primary language for every aspect of society, Latin and Greek, but also associated with this their own thought system that affected how they considered the faith. The Eastern Church lived in a heavily philosophical culture that had grown from great figures such as Socrates, Plato, and Aristotle, and this area continued to be the philosophical centre of Europe even after it was incorporated into the Roman empire. While there was a desire in this environment to investigate and discuss theology, the philosophical climate did not demand clear answers to questions and was content to leave much in the realm of mystery.

The Western Church took a rather different approach, in line with a different cultural attitude to knowledge. The Latin mind was less interested in thinking for its own sake, appreciating more the results of that thought in politics or law and seeking an end point to discussions. This affected the development of Western theology from Augustine's time onwards, with its nature being far more definite than the more mystical theology found in the East. One aspect of this was the different words available in each language, a good example being the concept of the three-in-one godhead. The Eastern Church worked with Aristotle's words *ousia* and *hypostasis*, which indicate what something is and how it appears in quite subtle ways; the Western Church often ended up using *substantia* and *persona*, more concrete terms – substance and persons – that are more dangerous when applied to a God who is essentially spirit.

As theology developed in the West, this approach increasingly led to a definitive and extensive systematic theology that can be considered for its strengths and weaknesses, while the continuing approach to knowledge in Western culture gave rise to reasoned critiques of the developing doctrines of the church.

Alongside the development of this new stream of theology based on this different method from the earlier, Greek-thinking church, there was a new approach to the leadership of the church centred on the office of the bishop of Rome and a progression towards papal theology. Crucial to this change was the collapse of the Western Roman empire from the fifth century onwards, which resulted in a fragile and fragmented political landscape with one key unifying factor: the church, with the bishop of Rome at its head. In the split of the Roman empire, four Patriarchs were located in the East and only one in the West.

Certain stages in the elevation of the role of the bishop of Rome within the Western Church began before the break-up of the Western Roman empire. By the Council of Constantinople, there was a movement to ascribe a *primacy* to the bishop of Rome based on the succession from St Peter. This was still in question – hence the bishop of Rome did not himself attend this Council – but, even where it was accepted, this primacy was very different from any notion of *supremacy*. Primacy indicated an idea of first among equals rather than a headship over the other Patriarchs. The idea of supremacy developed once the Roman empire collapsed in the West and the two halves progressed down very different routes, the East retaining a close link between church and empire for the next thousand years, the West entering into a new situation in which the bishop of Rome took on a political role as a secular lord that included crowning emperors, and therefore claimed a worldly authority in addition to an authority in the church.

This political element was important for the church throughout the medieval period. It affected how other rulers, who played important roles in the faith position of their citizens, related to the bishop of Rome; it meant that the popes engaged with wider socio-political issues, even undertaking military activity – this not only in the Crusades, but in other conflicts with secular rulers; and it would create a different claim to authority, since the lordly aspect that pertained to secular dominion affected the leadership role of popes in the church.

The church in the West thus experienced a radical shift from the early centuries both in how it thought and in how it operated, the two areas that would ultimately lead to an official split or schism in the church in 1054, when the Catholic and Orthodox Churches separated over the authority of the pope and the nature of the procession of the Holy Spirit, the latter resulting from linguistic and theological developments in the West away from the position defined in the Creed of 381.

THE CHALLENGE OF AUGUSTINE

Augustine of Hippo will feature in a couple of the chapters to come, particularly those on grace and faith/belief/works, but for now the focus is on the impact of his writings on the nature of the developing church. An important part of any consideration of Augustine must be his place in the history of Western thought. Before him, there were very few significant writers in Latin, given that the centre of Christianity was in the East, where Greek was used.

Augustine writes a huge amount of significant material on a range of topics that challenge people's understanding of God, humankind, salvation, and the church, among other things. Much of what he writes, particularly in his later works, is not clearly in line with the previous teaching of the church, yet is scripturally based and thus fully worthy of consideration. The problem that ultimately results for the West is the proximity of Augustine's writings to the fall of the Western Roman empire, which leads to a poverty of theological reflection for several centuries.[3]

---

3   The "Dark Ages" were not without sparks of light, such as Boethius, Gregory the Great, and John Erigena – the latter being involved in the first of the medieval renaissances – but there was a shortage of extensive theological discussion before the end of the eleventh century.

With the Greek language largely falling into disuse in the West, the sources for the study of theology were few and were certainly dominated by Jerome's translation of the Bible in the Vulgate and Augustine's works. Augustine thus becomes the central lens through which many areas of theology are considered from this point on, without a strong initial critical engagement. His writings do not seem ever to have had much of an impact on Eastern theology, owing to linguistic and cultural differences; the clearest example of this would be Augustine's work on the Trinity, which approached the whole concept from a different angle and led the Western Church to misunderstand and then misinterpret even the creedal teaching on the godhead.

Augustine is thus a defining voice in the West and some of his work relates to the nature of the church and its relationship with society as it moved into the Middle Ages, thereby setting up some of the problems that would be considered in the period of the Reformation.

At the core of the teachings that would change the nature of the church is Augustine's extension of the concept of original sin. The earlier church had consistently accepted that humankind as a whole had been corrupted as a result of the first sin recorded in the Bible so that all were in need of grace for salvation, received through the work of Christ. Alongside this, however, was a teaching of original grace that would cover the effects of original sin in infants and the young, so that those who died before reaching an age of responsibility were covered by that grace. This position is shown mostly clearly in a short pamphlet by Gregory of Nyssa called *On Infants' Early Deaths*, in which Gregory reassures his readers that children who die early in life receive new life because of the grace of God.

Augustine extends the concept of original sin to include what may be called original guilt, namely that even infants are guilty of sin and under the judgment of God as a result, meaning that (as one chapter in his book, *On the Merits and Forgiveness of Sins, and on the Baptism of Infants*, is entitled) "unbaptized infants [are] damned, but most lightly". To a certain extent the change is not fundamentally significant, because both positions require God's grace to overcome the effects of original sin. Whereas, in the earlier church, this grace is indicated as common until a person becomes responsible for their own sin, Augustine locates it in the mystery of baptism, in which the effects of original sin that condemn a person are washed away. The focus of both is that election is through the unearned grace of God, and is not conditional on the merit of either the life or the beliefs of the individual.

One of the key aspects of Augustine's teaching that builds on this is the relationship of the phases of grace in the continuing salvation of a person. The fact that someone has received this first grace, either as an infant or as an adult, does not guarantee their eternal salvation, but this is only the first step and is purely the work of God. Two relevant terms are usually applied to this, the first being "prevenient grace", which simply means the grace that comes before any movement of a person towards God and shows that preparation for salvation is necessarily dependent on God's first action; the second is "efficient grace", which is the grace that effects salvation in the individual. For infants, these two are combined in the parents' presentation and then the act of baptism; for adults, there can be discernible preparatory steps before a person receives salvation.

These must be followed up, however, in what is called "cooperating grace", which helps a person to persevere through the rest of their life, when their will, awakened and empowered by grace, continues to live for God. Everybody will still sin after baptism, but these sins are not necessarily sufficient to tear a person from their state of salvation. Augustine uses the terms "venial" and "mortal" to distinguish between sins that stain a person and those that kill them spiritually, with the expectation that most people will commit only the former type of sin after baptism.

Augustine also develops the concept of the intermediate state that the church had consistently taught. This is based on the dominant teaching of the New Testament that there will be a judgment day at the end of time when all will be raised and divided into those who are granted eternal life and those who are not. This leaves a time gap between death and judgment, which the early church had not sought to define clearly but understood as a place of waiting. Augustine is part of one line of thought that saw this as a time of purification for those who would go to glory, cleansing them of the stains of sins committed after baptism.

This is a vital stage in the development of the concept of purgatory, which would grow in importance largely for political and social reasons in the centuries after Augustine. During Augustine's lifetime, Christianity was growing as a force in the Roman empire but was far from absolute dominance in the religious sphere – there was an anti-Christian emperor in power early in Augustine's life, the emperor Julian. In the following centuries, as Western Europe grew politically weaker and more fragmented, the church grew more powerful throughout every aspect of society and gradually through various types of mission formed what is known as Christendom.

The result for most areas of Western Europe was a different role for the church in relation to its members. The people generally followed the religion of their king or lord, placing their faith in these leaders and in the god that they worshipped. In our modern, predominantly literate, society, it can be difficult to understand the nature of Christianity in times such as Dark Ages Europe. With Augustine's theology dominant, all infants would be baptized and receive grace to overcome the effects of original sin. It was considered abuse not to baptize an infant on this understanding of original sin because their eternal salvation would be threatened.

This means that all people enter the church, receive salvation grace, and receive the Holy Spirit when they are infants owing to this prevenient grace of God, received through the faith of their parents. One result of Augustine's teaching through this later history of the church is a concentration not on people becoming Christians, receiving first grace, but on continuing as Christians through cooperating or persevering grace. Missions continue to non-Christian peoples, but within the church the focus is on living out the faith with the assistance of grace. As long as people do not commit mortal sins – murder, adultery – their eternal salvation is not in doubt, but the venial sins that they continue to succumb to result, in Augustine's understanding, in a harsher time in purgatory before they are given resurrection life.

When these teachings are combined with a society that was largely illiterate and agricultural, with little social mobility and often a short lifespan, we can begin to understand why the church's concentration was on encouraging faith in its members, faith in God and in his church, rather than on promoting deep beliefs in each individual. The beliefs of the church were taught in catechetical classes, but the long-term effects of these seem to have been fairly minimal. It was important that the church had solid beliefs and that the people had faith in the church's beliefs, whether they could understand them or not. There was no opposition to a person seeking a greater intensity of faith, but for this they would need training and time to devote themselves to it, and such was available by joining a monastic community, and these were open to all.

Augustine's teachings on original sin, baptismal grace, and the need to persevere in grace until death solidified Christian identity in the church for the medieval period, and once Christianity had become the religion of the kingdoms of Western Europe these together changed the role of the church from seeking to save people for Christ to retaining them in Christ. The church was seen to be the body of Christ in which dwelt the Spirit of Christ, guiding the body and its leaders into truth. Salvation was secure when in communion with the invisible church, which became synonymous with the visible church; outside this communion (in a state of excommunication), there could be no assurance of forgiveness.

THE MEDIEVAL CHURCH

The church was thus set up to be the guardian of the faith of its members, protecting them and encouraging them throughout their lives in the power of the Holy Spirit that dwells in the church and in individual Christians. There is little wrong with such an understanding of church – indeed, we will see that this is what the major reformers called the church back to – yet by the sixteenth century there was not only a need for reform but such a strong call for it that some would risk leaving the structures of the church in order to effect the necessary change.

What were the problems with the church that allowed, even compelled, people to seek salvation outside its walls? Some of the factors will be left to later chapters, particularly those concerning attitudes to Scripture and the teaching on key themes such as grace and faith. Here we will look at two themes that created conditions for a break with church authority, one in society and one in the church itself.

We start with society and the very possibility of questioning the church in any aspect of its teaching, given its role in the preservation and then expansion of knowledge in Western Europe. For many centuries, the church was the only vehicle for acquiring and investigating knowledge, in monastic and cathedral schools, and then from the twelfth century in the first universities, which, particularly in Northern Europe, were heavily influenced by the church.

Philosophy and theology, which are naturally closely related, were studied under the church, with a constant awareness of the dangers of "free" thinking given the struggles of the early church with a range of teachings that were ultimately deemed heretical. To safeguard against new false ideas, the church allied Scripture closely with the writings of the Church Fathers, who were seen to provide a reliable understanding of the gospel. The importance of this unity of Scripture and tradition was highlighted in the early twelfth century when a philosopher–theologian called Peter Abelard wrote a book called *Sic et Non* (which simply translates as "Yes and No"), in which he analyzed the writings of the Church Fathers on a range of subjects and showed that there were strong contrasts and even apparent contradictions in their views. This book was attacked not for inaccuracy, but because it undermined people's faith in the teachings of the church.

Over the next couple of centuries, more sources of knowledge came into Western European thought via the rediscovery of ancient texts and the arrival of Jewish and Arab ideas. For the most part, the church was able to continue its protection of the faith, partly through its influence in universities and partly by the threat of excommunication, the power of which should not be undervalued in a society where one's eternal identity was often prioritized over the temporal one, given how little the latter could be changed.

The church took major steps to protect the faith of its members, beginning with the foundation of the Dominican monastic order in 1216. St Dominic travelled into southern France and found that a new version of an old heresy (Catharism, an updated form of Gnosticism, which emphasized the spirit over the body) was rife in the area and that churches were not equipped to defend Christian teaching. The Dominican Order, or the Order of Friars Preaching, was established to train preachers who could travel around Europe and counter false ideas wherever they were found.

It was from the Dominican Order that the Papal Inquisition and later the Spanish Inquisition (did anyone expect that in this book?) developed. Given that I am about to write something mildly positive about the Inquisitions, it is important at the outset to clarify that this is no defence of the use of torture and other violence that was carried out as part of their examination of people suspected of false teachings. Many of the acts carried out by the Inquisitors and on their orders were horrific. With this in mind, it is worth recognizing that the intention behind their actions was a defence of the purity of the faith of whole communities, whose eternal salvation was deemed to be at risk if false teachings were allowed to continue and even to spread. While the church of today must condemn many of the methods used by the Inquisitions, we can be challenged by their motivation to guard a true faith for communities and consider what the right steps to take might be in this regard.

The growth of the universities with their critical discussions and the discovery (or rediscovery) of additional sources of knowledge were combined with a greater confidence in humanity and its ability to achieve and progress that was displayed in the movement known as the Renaissance. From the twelfth to the fifteenth century, these threads wove together to allow a new critical attitude to develop even to the church. Augustine taught a rather pessimistic view of human nature as it resulted from original sin, and the importance of the grace communicated by God through the church made people reticent about critiquing this spiritual institution and its leaders.

One of the most interesting early proofs of scepticism regarding church authority comes from Guibert of Nogent, who in the early twelfth century wrote a work that highlighted major issues with the church's teaching on relics – the most famous part of which is probably his observation that two separate churches each claimed to possess the severed head of John the Baptist. In mainland Europe, particular problems with the church continued to be commented on – such as monasteries that fell into bad practices – largely because the church was responsible for the salvation of its members and for protecting society from spiritual attack. But the powerful threat of excommunication and a continuing respect for authority combined to lessen the impact of the critiques.

England was somewhat different, for a variety of reasons: its place on the edge of the political map; less respect for office (most notably shown in the events surrounding Magna Carta); and the greater independence of the church. On the last point, the appointment of officials from the Archbishop of Canterbury down had been the responsibility of the kings of England for many centuries, which left little space for the papacy to intrude into church matters in England.

This greater independence on the part of England was best displayed in two separate, strong attacks on the church towards the end of the fourteenth century. The better known of these came from John Wycliffe, most famous for his inspiration for the translation of the Bible, but this was an example of his central point that queried the nature of the authority of the pope. Wycliffe was not seeking the overthrow of the church structure of his time, recognizing the pope as the "highest vicar that Christ has here in earth"; however, he showed that the measure of how this was being carried out should be faithfulness to the humble life of Christ, rather than any kind of worldly authority. The popes of Wycliffe's time seemed to have forgotten that one of their titles was "the servant of servants of Christ" (*servus servorum Christi*). If Wycliffe had lived in mainland Europe, he would probably have been brought to trial for his views; living in England, he was protected by the crown against some of the most extreme challenges from the church.

A second critique of the church in England was an allegorical poem written by William Langland towards the end of the fourteenth century, entitled *Piers Plowman*. This satirizes many aspects of England at the time, but the church does come in for some particularly pointed attacks. Here are just a few examples:

> *I saw some that said they had sought saints:*
> *Yet in each tale that they told their tongue turned to lies*
> *More than to tell truth it seemed by their speech.*
> *Hermits, a heap of them with hooked staves,*
> *Were going to Walsingham and their wenches too...*[4]
> *I found there friars of all the four orders,*
> *Preaching to the people for profit to themselves,*
> *Explaining the Gospel just as they liked.*

---

4   For those who missed it, hermits were not supposed to have "wenches" accompanying them anywhere.

Those disliking alliteration will naturally react against texts like these, but I hope that all can sense the strength of such popular writing in giving voice to criticisms of a revered part of society. These verses highlight one major problem for the church in the medieval period, which was control over church appointments. We have already noted that the papacy did not appoint archbishops of Canterbury (the case of Thomas Becket being a classic example of this) or other offices in England, but likewise appointment to major and minor positions in the church elsewhere in Europe could depend on the favour of kings and local rulers. Considering the landed estates that came with some church offices, it is perhaps unsurprising that they were not always sought by the most spiritual of men.

There were regular attempts to reform the church, most notably during a period known as the Conciliar Papacy in the early fifteenth century, when several abuses were highlighted and steps taken to correct them. But the effects of reforms depended on their enactment by local authorities, both inside and outside the church.

The fact that the church exists in a sinful world and its leaders and members are sinful people means that no "perfect church" will ever exist on earth. The growing middle classes of medieval Europe did expect to see the church acting when abuses were apparent, however. Crucially, the Western Church was seen to be held together by the pope, the heir of St Peter, on which rock Christ had promised to build his church. Once there were problems with the papacy itself, the church was in real danger.

One incident that weakened the authority of the bishop of Rome concerned what was known as the Donation of Constantine, supposedly a fourth-century document in which the emperor Constantine bestowed considerable temporal and spiritual authority on the pope of the time, Sylvester I. This had been used for centuries by the papacy to defend a lordly relationship between popes and secular rulers, but the document was shown by Lorenzo Valla in the fifteenth century to be a forgery. Two further examples are sufficient to show why confidence in the papacy was so low by the sixteenth century that people felt obliged to leave the visible church despite the inevitable sentence of excommunication.

The first is known as the Papal Schism, when the rulers of Europe split over the choice of pope. There had been controversies before over who was the rightful pope, most notably between Urban II and the "antipope" Clement III at the end of the eleventh century. In 1378, following the return to Rome of the pope after the Babylonian Captivity of the Papacy at Avignon, the relationship between Pope Urban VI and the cardinals was such that they elected a rival pope, Clement VII. The result was two claimants to the title for the next forty years, with the exception of a few years at the end when a new pope was elected to resolve the dispute, resulting in three popes for a short time. While the church did resolve the matter, the authority of the papal office was damaged, and for a time after the union of the church, the person of the pope was less important and councils of the church increased in significance.

The second example was the election and rule from 1492 of Pope Alexander VI, a man born as Rodrigo Borgia. The Borgia family are now infamous for their desire for power and use of almost any means to secure it. Alexander VI was probably elected as the result of simony – buying the votes of the cardinals – and lived more as a Renaissance prince than as leader of the church. He was known to have multiple children, obviously an issue given his vow of celibacy, and appointed one of his sons a cardinal in 1493. That such a man could become the heir of St Peter necessarily weakened the respect that the office of pope would naturally command in the medieval understanding of the church.

REFORMING THE CHURCH

There is no doubt that by the early sixteenth century the church was in need of reform, but the question was on what basis reforms should be implemented and what their goal was. This section will look at five broad themes relating to church that were present in reforming thought – each of which could be broken down into subsections if there were space – and later chapters will pick up on aspects of these as groups worked through their approach to Scripture, grace, faith, and other concepts.

Luther

Luther's initial agenda, which continued to be the driving force in the movement he led, was to reform the Catholic Church back to what it had historically been, liberating it from secular influences and power interests that had corrupted elements of the church. The famous 95 Theses that are generally held to be the starting point of the Reformation show a desire not to overturn the church but to correct elements of teaching. Here are just a couple of examples:

> *6. The Pope has no power to remit any guilt, except by declaring and warranting it to have been remitted by God; or at most by remitting cases reserved for himself, in which cases, if his power were despised, guilt would certainly remain.*

*38. The remission, however, imparted by the Pope is
by no means to be despised, since it is, as I have said,
a declaration of the Divine remission.*

In the early years of his transformed life, Luther appeals to the
pope to rescue the faith from other forces in the church and
attends disputations to discuss elements of Christian teaching
in order to secure reforms. While Luther's language changes
in regard to the institution of the papacy and to the popes
themselves, he, his colleague Melanchthon, and his followers
continue to be involved in discussions aimed at preserving
unity. Most notable among these, although Luther himself was
not present, was the meeting at Regensburg in 1541 between
the Lutheran Confession and the Catholic Church that
produced a book of articles, including one on justification.

While the structures and some of the practices of medieval
Catholicism receive harsh criticism from Luther, the concept
of the spiritual entity that is the church is largely upheld, since
much of this results from the work of Augustine of Hippo,
who had been so formative in the nature and doctrines of the
Western Church – Luther had taught Augustine as well as the
Bible in the university.

Luther retains a strong sacramental theology at the core
of his understanding of church, if not of salvation. While he
does not hold to the sacramental nature of all seven Catholic
sacraments, he does keep two as full sacraments – baptism
and the Lord's Supper – and teaches the importance of the
right practices of penance and marriage with appropriate
understanding of the grace at work in each. Luther changes
the teaching on baptism very little, and writes as much against
the Anabaptists (rebaptizers) as he does against the Catholic
Church on this point. While he rejects the doctrine of

transubstantiation as a corruption of people's understanding of the Lord's Supper based on the work of Aristotle, Luther is keen to uphold the real presence of Christ in the bread and wine and writes extensively against both Zwingli and the Anabaptists on this.

Related to this sacramental theology, of course, are Luther's ideas on the leadership of the church, including the priesthood. The concept of the "priesthood of all believers", based on Luther, is a core part of any Reformation study. Luther certainly taught this very clearly in his letter *Concerning the Ministry* to the people of Prague in 1520:

> *Let us now show from the work of priests that all*
> *Christians are equally priests ... when we give the*
> *word to anyone, we cannot deny anything to them*
> *that is related to being a priest.*

This is a short fragment of a long document asserting the equality of all Christians in being considered priests and doing the work of God. There is some beautiful writing here, but we must consider the purpose of the document rather than simply treating it neutrally. Luther is writing to encourage the people of Bohemia to throw off their ties to the papacy and celebrate their independent spirit in the religious as in other spheres. The letter ultimately fails in this, since, after a favourable initial reception, Bohemian society stays within the Catholic fold and begins to criticize this German novelty.

Elsewhere in his works, Luther writes positively about the functional value of ordained priests, as long as they are not understood to be higher than others or to have any greater natural worth. In his work *On the Sacrament of Penance*, Luther writes that "[o]ne should observe and not despise the established orders of authority, but do not make the mistake of thinking that the sacrament and its effects count for more if they are given by a bishop or a pope than if they are given by a priest or a lay person". This is applied to the process of forgiveness during confession, in which Luther consistently asserts that forgiveness is by faith and from God, but that the words of the priest play a part in the assurance of forgiveness that a person receives. When explaining the 95 Theses, Luther writes on similar lines:

> So as a general rule we are not sure of the remission
> of guilt except through the judgment of the priest,
> and not even through him unless you believe in
> Christ who has promised, "Whatever you shall loose,
> etc." [Matt. 16:19]. Moreover, as long as we are
> uncertain, there is no remission, since there is not yet
> remission for us… Therefore, God's remission effects
> grace, but the priest's remission brings peace, which
> is both the grace and gift of God, since it is faith in
> actual remission and grace.

In addition, Luther wrote extensively against the various Anabaptist groups who would follow the teachings of anyone they considered to be a prophet, however much this contrasted with a traditional understanding of the faith. Luther retained a strongly sacramental, historically influenced view of the church, which meant that he regarded it as in need of great reform because of some of the historical, political, and theological corruptions that he saw affecting it in his time, but it was a reforming project rather than the reboot that the Anabaptists often sought.

This look at Luther's views on the church is somewhat longer than the following studies because Luther sat in this middle position, critiquing the current form of the church while accepting some elements and also seeking to counter what he considered extreme voices that sought to deny all the contemporary understandings of the church.

Anabaptists

We have little evidence left from the Anabaptists. The main sources we have are the Schleitheim Confession composed by the Swiss Anabaptists in 1527 and the writings of Menno Simons, a Catholic priest turned Anabaptist, who wrote a series of works on a range of theological subjects. Simons left the Catholic Church in the mid-1530s, and was thus part of a second wave of Anabaptism already seeking to reform the movement.

With regard to the church, as in most areas, Anabaptist groups are considered part of a "Radical Reformation" that sought almost a complete new beginning for the church, set apart from everything associated with late medieval Catholicism. The twin new authorities were Scripture and the prophet (a term heavily used in Anabaptist groups), with the balance between these two varying from place to place.

One of the most significant early influences of Anabaptism in the Reformation period came at Wittenberg during the time when Karlstadt was leading the reformation of the church and the city in Luther's absence. A group known as the "Zwickau prophets" came from the city of that name in Saxony; these men – Nicholas Storch, Thomas Drechsel, and Marcus Thomae or Stübner – had been expelled because of their teaching against infant baptism and their claim to immediate divine revelation by the Spirit of the destruction of the priests and the end of the world. They taught that the church comprised those people who had the Holy Spirit inside them, the Spirit being their sole teacher and something that had no connection either to Christ or to the Bible.

This group were highly influential both religiously and politically, since their teaching against authority was not just popular with those who perceived abuses within the church but could also be applied to wider society. When they were moved on from Wittenberg, Karlstadt's work both while he was in the city and after his own expulsion was influenced by their thought, moderated in his case by his knowledge of the Bible and theology.

The point at issue with early Anabaptist groups was the ability of an accepted prophet to determine the interpretation of Scripture (if, unlike the Zwickau prophets, a group continued to hold to the importance of Scripture), with the emphasis often on the role of the Spirit in the individual as an authority in itself. A second early incident in Münster showed up this problem. In 1534, the city was taken over by radical Anabaptists who declared it to be the New Jerusalem, a movement led successively by the prophets Jan Mathijs and Jan Bockelson. These instituted a new society that blended church and state, with the punishment for sinners being death – and sins ranging from blasphemy and adultery down to complaining. Bockelson also had a vision that led him to introduce polygamy, with fifty people being executed for resisting the new kingdom that he was introducing. Although this experiment lasted less than two years, it played a major part in the response of the church to the Anabaptist approach.

Before we move on to Simons and more moderate Anabaptism, we should mention two further factors that affected how other figures viewed these disparate groups. The first concerns infant baptism, which Luther and others defended as scriptural and part of the historic faith of the church but which was denied by the Anabaptists. Given the enduring view of sin inherited from Augustine, this denial of baptism to infants cut them off from grace in the view of other reformers (including Catholic, of course) and restricted the church only to adults who could demonstrate belief.

The second factor is the complete separation of church and state that was often part of Anabaptist teaching, where other reforms held that the church was one aspect of a person's wider identity in society. In the early sixteenth century, when identity was more congruent across and transcended different parts of a person's life, the divorce of church from political or social ties was seen as divisive by others, while the Anabaptists strongly supported it as a means of guarding the faith against pressures from factors outside the church.

In contrast to the more radical examples of Anabaptism, the writings of Menno Simons show a dedication to the authority of Scripture and a desire to instil this as the foundation of all thought on the Christian faith. While there is some antichrist language, in many of his works Simons is seeking to reach out to other Christians to encourage them to reform their ideas in the light of Scripture. Simons does not write at length on what he considers the church to be, but does address excommunication in three separate works, which of course is highly relevant. In one of these, he writes:

> Brothers, understand correctly that we do
> not excommunicate or expel anyone from the
> communion of brothers except for those who have
> already separated and expelled themselves from
> communion with Christ either by false doctrines or
> by improper conduct.

This is very reasonable. But the question that was naturally asked at the time of the Reformation, by the Catholics, Luther, and Calvin (among others), was this: given that you seem to have cut yourself off from the historic teachings of the church, on what basis can you deem a doctrine false or a conduct improper? The individual church leader becomes the authority on the interpretation of Scripture and the decision concerning the extent to which they would use the teachings of the church, if at all. If the Bible were a simple, clear textbook, there would be no problem. But the history of the church from its earliest times shows that correct Christian teaching is hard to maintain with all the cultural, societal, philosophical, and linguistic challenges around, and the biblical writings themselves are open to what the church has considered misinterpretation by those who mean and seek to do good.

Anabaptism continued to pose its challenge to the church to reform further by the "headline" figures – Luther, Zwingli, and Calvin – had desired. It was not a movement that was ever united, except on the point of adult baptism, given that the teachings of each church would depend on the approach of its leader to the respective roles of and attitudes to the Bible and the Spirit. This challenge would be particularly formative in the Dutch Reformed churches, in later Anglican development, and of course in the formation of the Baptist churches.

Calvin

One key element of Calvin's concept of salvation is his doctrine of election; of the people who God knows will inherit eternal life because of the grace they have received by faith. This relates more to what has been termed "the invisible church", but in considering the church Calvin writes almost exclusively about the visible church with regard to both the Catholic Church and the various movements that have departed from this by the time of his work. We will be looking here through the lens of the final version of Calvin's *Institutes of the Christian Religion*, written in the mid-1550s.

Calvin's concept of election comes from his understanding of sin and grace. In short, he taught that salvation is by grace alone, a grace that initially saves and then continues to allow the believer to persevere in faith through their life until death. Therefore, it is God who chooses (the Latin *electio* simply means "to choose") who will be saved because it is his power alone that saves. This is tied to the fact that God is present throughout all time and thus is with a person at their death as he is with them at their birth and at every point in between. Given this fact of the nature of God, he necessarily knows whether I – having persevered in faith – will be saved at my death or not, because he is already there. Calvin follows the approach of all great theologians in getting his ideas of God right first before moving on to other areas.

When considering the church, Calvin is very clear that no Christian should seek to leave it because it is the body of Christ, despite the fact that some members of the church – even the leaders – may fall into various sins. Leaving the church because of the people is not an option for Calvin, but leaving a visible church that does not teach the gospel is not leaving the church, because the teaching shows that it is not what it claims to be. There is thus the invisible church that comprises the elect, and the visible church that teaches the faith and is in need of reform, a reform that includes its structures because Calvin believed that the nature of Catholic Church leadership was not in line with biblical models.

One line of Calvin's thought closely follows the later work of Augustine, and regarding the church it emphasizes the necessity for humility, faith, and obedience to God for its members and leaders. Calvin recognizes that those who are not selected for salvation can have an experience of God's grace that appears similar to that received by true members of the church, but argues that it is of a different order in the work of God. This means that believers should always ensure that they are relying on God and not on themselves, since the assurance that is available to the Christian is not one based on personal experiences, faith, or actions, but only ever on the work and promises of God. Here is a fairly lengthy (yet still edited) section in which Calvin talks about this:

> I am aware that some cannot understand how
> faith is acknowledged in a reprobate [not one of the
> elect] when Paul declares that it is one of the fruits
> of election, and yet the difficulty is easily solved.
> Although only those who are chosen for salvation
> are enlightened into faith and truly feel the power of
> the Gospel, yet experience shows that the reprobate
> are sometimes affected in a way so similar to the
> elect that even in their own judgment there is no
> difference between them. ... Should someone object
> that believers do not have a stronger testimony
> to assure them of their adoption, I answer that,
> although there is a great resemblance and affinity
> between God's elect and those who for a time receive
> a fading faith, yet only the elect have that full
> assurance that Paul extols by which they are enabled
> to cry, "Abba, Father".

*God effectually seals in the elect the grace of
his adoption in order that it may be sure and
steadfast. But there is nothing to prevent an
inferior operation of the Spirit from working in
the reprobate. Meanwhile, believers are taught to
examine themselves carefully and humbly, in case a
worldly security should creep in and take the place
of assurance of faith. … I do not deny that God
illumines the minds of some reprobates to the extent
that they recognize his grace; but he distinguishes
between this conviction and the particular testimony
which he gives to his elect … When he shows himself
favourable to them, it is not as if he has truly
rescued them from death and taken them under his
protection. … In this way we dispose of the objection
that, if God truly displays his grace, it must endure
for ever. There is nothing inconsistent in the fact that
he enlightens some with a present sense of grace,
which afterwards proves to be temporary.*

For Calvin, the church and salvation are purely the works of
God, and it is the role of humans to be humbly obedient. Once
the human voice or action becomes dominant, one should be
wary. A famous example of this in Calvin's work concerns sung
worship in church, which Calvin does not quite outlaw, but he
does state that "songs composed merely to tickle and delight
the ear are unbecoming to the majesty of the Church, and can
only be most displeasing to God", since free expression is liable
to human corruption in communication and people can lose
the meaning of songs through the distraction of musical forms.
While one may not agree with Calvin's views on sung worship,
the principle that leads him to this position is challenging in

its desire to ensure that everything rests on the work of God rather than on the results of the efforts of sinful humanity.

This links well to his views on the visible church or churches present in his time, and the critique of the human authorities in the Catholic Church; particularly papal authority, but also the theological authority arising out of the universities, which overtook the work of God by his Spirit in the church. This does not mean that the visible church becomes worthless – such a thought would be horrifying to Calvin, as the following passage shows:

> *As it is now our purpose to discuss the visible*
> *Church, let us learn from her single title of Mother*
> *how useful, indeed how necessary the knowledge of*
> *her is, because there is no other means of entering*
> *into life unless the church conceives us in the womb*
> *and gives us birth, unless she nourishes us at her*
> *breasts, and, in short, keeps us under her charge*
> *and government until, divested of mortal flesh,*
> *we become like the angels (Mt. 22:30). ...Beyond*
> *the pale of the Church we cannot hope for any*
> *forgiveness of sins or salvation.*

Calvin argues that, through some of the structures of the papacy, the devil has gained great influence, and states that "it is obvious that we do not at all deny that churches remain under his tyranny". The extent of human authority affects the ability of a church to dedicate itself completely to God. In this, Calvin critiques the Anabaptists along with the Catholics for putting themselves above Scripture and the church in their teachings and their models of church, commenting on "the conduct of the Anabaptists, who, acknowledging no assembly of Christ unless conspicuous in all respects for angelic perfection, under the pretence of zeal overthrow everything which tends to edification".

Calvin's concept of church thus rests on his concepts of God and of sinful humanity, with the mark of a true church being an absolute dependence on God and his revelation in Scripture and in the church to which the Spirit is given.

The Anglican Church

Owing to the nature of the English Reformation, coming as it did from a long-standing tradition of critiquing authority and triggered by Henry's marriage problems, the basis for considering the nature of the church is different from those we have looked at thus far. This is no reform based on corruptions either of doctrines or of a wider attitude to Scripture or Spirit, but a reality driven by a moral and political dispute that then requires implementation. This study will focus on the first stage of the English Reformation, that partly overseen by Thomas Cranmer as Archbishop of Canterbury.

The one key factor in the nature of the English church after the Act of Supremacy was the loss of papal authority over religion in England. It was largely the danger of a challenge to this that led to the dissolution of the monasteries, since the members of these would have a devotion to their order and from that to the pope as the head of the Catholic Church (although the financial benefit to the crown cannot have harmed the case for this action). Beyond this, there were no absolutes forced on the nature of the new church.

The fact that the king was the head of the church and the head of his country had an implication: the church was to be for the English. By the mid-1530s, a variety of views were already present in the country, although the dominant strain of Christian religion was still Catholicism. Alongside this were teachings both from the Lutheran Reformation and from scholars related to Swiss reformers, which began to gain importance during the 1530s, particularly in Cambridge through the influence of Thomas Cranmer, who had taught there.

The dominant force while he lived was Henry VIII – a notable theologian in his own right, most clearly in his response to the teachings of Martin Luther against the sacraments, for which he was given the title "Defender of the Faith". In the middle of the 1530s, Thomas Cromwell was also powerful from a more reforming perspective, as we can see in the Injunctions of 1536 and 1538 that attacked core aspects of Catholic spirituality, such as relics and even the doctrine of purgatory. Henry withdrew his support for a more radical reformation toward the end of that decade, however, composing the Six Articles for the Anglican Church that supported the doctrine of transubstantiation, one of the few elements that all other Protestant groups were united in rejecting.

Henry's church was not simply Catholicism without the pope, as has sometimes been argued, although the dissolution of the monasteries was largely anti-papal in its intent because monasteries carried an allegiance through their communities to Rome. It is important in the history of Irish religion that Henry did not dissolve the monasteries there, despite adopting the title of king in relation to Ireland, as the preservation of the monasteries played an important role in the continuation of Catholic faith in Ireland.

The reform was certainly more radical than just the removal of the pope, in the reduction of emphasis on certain sacraments and in attacks on elements of Catholic spirituality that were deemed mere superstition. During Henry's lifetime the reform was heavily influenced by the king's more traditional approach. Once Henry died and Cranmer took a greater lead, we can see a stronger influence of Reformation principles, most clearly in the 42 Articles that were published in 1553 (and which formed the basis for the later 39 Articles that continue to underpin Anglican doctrine today).

The 42 Articles and Cranmer's Book of Common Prayer (1549) show a new approach that is certainly more Protestant than that found during Henry's reign, but not one that is greatly dominated by any particular strain of Protestant thought. A good example of this is the approach to the Lord's Supper, which has wonderfully subtle wording that allows those holding to a real presence of Christ and those with a much more symbolic understanding to come to the same table – note the phrase "in these holy mysteries" as important in this:

> *Grant us therefore, gracious Lord, so to eat the flesh*
> *of your dear son Jesus Christ and to drink his blood*
> *in these holy mysteries that we may continually*
> *dwell in him and he in us, that our sinful bodies may*
> *be made clean by his body and our souls washed*
> *through his most precious blood.*

The tie between church and state is important in many ways, one of which is the unity of the kingdom. Given the notable weakness of the Tudor dynasty from the failure of Henry's marriage to Catherine of Aragon onwards, having a form of Christianity that could unite the people despite the presence of followers of Catholicism, Lutheran teachings, and ideas from the Swiss reformers was an essential element of any sense of national identity. Religion in this period is a core element at the heart of society, and disunity in this sphere would indicate a weakness in the whole. Without a strong theological basis for reform, the Anglican Church could seek to include different viewpoints. This would continue to be the case during the Elizabethan settlement after Mary's attempt to reinstate Catholicism.

Catholic Reformation

The church was in need of some kind of reform by the beginning of the sixteenth century, as it had been before – we have noted the series of reforms that were enacted during the Conciliar Papacy early in the fifteenth century – so any idea that the church was immovable is incorrect. The question for the church was how the need for reforms should be recognized and then acted upon.

The Catholic concept of the church was that it was the body of Christ in which dwelt the Spirit of Christ – a reasonable idea in the light of Scripture. That it was filled with fallible humans was no doubt true, but, just as the Spirit reliably inspired Scripture through human writers, so the Catholic Church believed that the Spirit could guide the church despite the weaknesses of its members and even leaders. A good example of this is the following passage from the Council of Sens in 1528:

> *The universal Church cannot fall into error, being led by the Spirit of truth dwelling in it for ever. Christ will remain with the Church until the end of the world ... [The Church] is taught by the same one Spirit to determine what is required by the changing circumstances of the times.*[5]

---

5   This seems to have been a relatively minor, local council and is not part of most Reformation histories, yet the power of this quote in what it says about the nature of the church shows that we should perhaps be more aware of its teachings.

There was thus a resistance to the idea of people who placed themselves outside the church (which in the Catholic understanding included not acknowledging the authority of the pope as the heir of St Peter) calling for reforms in the church. Luther initially used mainstream methods in publishing his theses and defending his theology in disputations with representatives of the Catholic Church, as did Zwingli in Zurich, but ultimately both believed that the scale of reform they demanded would not be carried through by the church. The closest that the church of the time came to some resolution was at Regensburg in 1541, when a book of agreed articles of faith was published, but two key issues – papal authority and transubstantiation – were missing from this, and attempts at maintaining unity were eventually abandoned.

The Catholic Church did reform at the Council of Trent (1545–63), but by this stage the Reformation was thirty years into its development and one can at times hear as much anti-Protestant thought in the decrees as constructive Catholic theology. The Council did not meet properly for eighteen years, being forced to move from Trent to Bologna and back, and of the twenty-five sessions that produced decrees, only eleven of them were substantially theological, with most of the remainder relating to opening, closing, and moving the Council.

The Council sought in its theology to establish the faith of the church through the centuries relating to Scripture, sin, justification, and grace through the sacraments, clarifying these by highlighting perceived errors in Protestant teachings. Thus the Council did not reform the theology of the church greatly. In each of the major sessions, however, there is extensive reform of the church in a second part of the decrees.

The first always deals with a major matter, such as the doctrine of original sin, but the longer second part reforms elements of church practice. In Session Five, which deals with Scripture, the reforms demand that there be qualified teachers of Scripture in all churches and monasteries since there has been a lack of people trained in theology to pass on the teaching of the church, particularly in poorer, parochial churches:

> *Let bishops be on their guard and not permit any one preach in their city and diocese unless they are known to them and have approved morals and doctrine, whether they are monks in name, living out of their monasteries and in obedience to their religious institute, or secular priests.*

> *As for churches whose annual revenues are small and where the number of clergy and laity is so small that a lectureship in theology cannot be conveniently maintained, let them at least have a master – to be chosen by the bishop with the advice of the chapter – to teach grammar freely to clerics and other poor scholars, so that they may afterwards, with God's blessing, pass on to the said study of sacred scripture.*

The decrees of the Council of Trent show an awareness that the critique of the church is valid at least with regard to some of its morality, the appointment and control of priests and even bishops, and the communication of the faith to congregations. But the idea that those outside the church can provide a critique goes against the continuing concept of the church, with the Council of Trent backing up the earlier statement from Sens:

*It is in the Church that we have the Bible, that
we have the gospel and that we have authentic
understanding of the gospel, or rather, the Church
itself is the gospel, written not with ink, but by the
Spirit of the living God and not on tablets of stone,
but on tablets of flesh of the heart.*

The key idea here is the "authentic understanding of the gospel", which calls us back to the earliest church, which had this as its major care in the light of attacks from within the church and from cultural and philosophical influences outside it.

CONCLUSION

It is important to start with the concept of the church because everything else flows from this: the view of and interpretation of Scripture, the development of Christian thought in various areas, and the application of this to the life of individuals and congregations. The church in Western Europe had a very particular history – especially with the single Patriarch and the lengthy Dark Ages that raised the role of the church in an individual's faith and spirituality – and the educational, social, and political developments of the medieval period created issues for the church that demanded reform.

It is interesting in this context to note that the church in the Eastern Roman empire did not suffer to the same extent from contamination of its form and ideas, and has never been through a similar experience of reformation. Because this empire continued for a thousand years after that of the West, albeit declining greatly in size, there was much greater continuity from the early church – this was also helped by the ongoing use of the Greek language. The structure of the church did not change, although some Patriarchates fell under Muslim control, and significant theological issues were dealt with in later general councils rather than being influenced by either an equivalent of the pope or the approach taken by the universities in the West.

The Catholic Church needed to be reformed – there were very few who disputed that. The question was on what grounds and in which areas reforms were needed. In almost every instance of reforming thought (and there were many subdivisions and even separate strands beyond those looked at in this chapter), there were different approaches that were applied and different doctrines that formed the foci. The vast majority – the more radical Anabaptists were the exception – were looking at a reform of the church back to its core faith as revealed in Scripture. We now turn to look at what this meant for their approach to the biblical writings.

Chapter Two

APPROACHES TO SCRIPTURE

It would seem logical when considering areas of Christianity to look at Scripture first, seeing that it is foundational to almost all approaches to the Christian faith. Yet the writings that form the Bible are not simple in themselves and do not automatically lead every reader to the same beliefs about God, humankind, and salvation. They require interpretation at various levels for different audiences and this is done in the church, or some form of church; hence the order of chapters in this book.

I love the Bible more than anything for how messy it is as a revelation of God and his work. On my study shelves I have a number of systematic theology books that break Christianity down into sections and deal with each in turn, providing some sort of conclusion about what we should believe and how we should act in the light of each study. The Bible doesn't do that. It is a collection of stories, letters, songs, laws, weird apocalyptic visions, an erotic love poem, and prophetic utterances without commentary on how a later reader should read these texts, because they were written at a certain time to a certain audience and thus have an internal purpose.

Things are not made easier in this respect by what we see when New Testament writers quote Old Testament passages. Firstly, we notice when we look back to the original passage that the wording is different and seems to be misquoted (it isn't, but we will come to that shortly).[6] Secondly, and perhaps more worrying, is that the New Testament writers do not always seem to use the Old Testament texts in the light of their original meaning and context, but pluck them out apparently just to support their arguments – something we are told in church that we should not do.

This study will follow the method of the previous chapter by looking at how the early church thought about and used Scripture, and then trace how this developed through the medieval period to produce a context in which it became one of the main battlegrounds between reforming groups in the early sixteenth century.

EARLY CHURCH

The Bible is such a core part of the Christian life today that it can be difficult to recognize that the church has not always had this definitive written source for its faith. The "canon" of Scripture – the books that make up the Old and New Testaments – was only agreed at the Council of Carthage in 419, which established the books for both the Western and the Eastern Church. The attitude to texts ultimately included in and excluded from this list of books changed through the early centuries of the church, however, with some consistently recognized as authoritative for the faith and others under some dispute.

---

6   As an example, Paul quotes Isaiah 45:23 in Romans 14:11, but the words are significantly different in the NIV translation.

For this study we must bear in mind a lesson from the nature of the early church. As we have seen, the chief goal of this church was the preservation and communication of the faith received from Christ and the apostles, uncorrupted by false teachers within the church or by cultural influences from outside. For most of the first 200 years of the church, the oral tradition – the gospel and associated stories passed down by word of mouth – was an authority in matters of faith at least as influential as written texts. At the end of the second century, Irenaeus of Lyon had a unique authority as a disciple of Polycarp of Smyrna, who in turn had been taught by the apostle John. As the distance between the early church and the apostles grew, there was a gradual move towards finding authority in the writings accepted by the church, primarily the four Gospels and many of the letters of Paul.

Old Testament

We should start, however, by looking at the Old Testament before we get on to the writings of the New. This should be a much easier study, except for the fact that there were two versions of the Old Testament scriptures in use – one in Hebrew and one in Greek (what is known as the Septuagint). The Greek version includes extra material: the seven books often known as the Apocrypha (Tobit, Judith, Wisdom, Ecclesiasticus, Baruch, I and II Maccabees) as well as additions to the books of Esther and Daniel.

The New Testament quotations from the Old Testament use the Septuagint – hence the differences in modern translations when one checks a quote in the Old Testament, because our translations of it come from the Hebrew – but there are no direct quotations from the additions to the Hebrew Bible. That said, there are no quotations from some of the books that are part of the Hebrew Bible, such as Esther, while the book of Jude uses as an authority a work known as the Assumption of Moses, which is a source outside even the longer version of the Old Testament.

The early church largely included the Apocrypha as part of its authoritative scriptures, quoting from these books in the same manner as from the rest of the Old Testament. This is unsurprising, seeing as the church was for the most part using Greek for its study of the Christian faith. There were some individuals who taught against this, generally those who had spent time in Palestine and were thus acquainted with Hebrew, such as Jerome, who is best known for translating the Bible into Latin. Origen of Alexandria is an interesting case as one who was familiar with the Jewish tradition and who therefore omitted the Apocryphal texts from his Old Testament canon, yet still used them as scriptures in his writing and defended their sacred value.

There continued to be some debate about the precise nature of these additions to the Hebrew scriptures in the early centuries, yet when writing theology all of them continued to be used as authorities for the faith even by a writer like Athanasius, who did not include them in his Old Testament canon. Ultimately, at the Council of Carthage, the Old Testament accepted by the church included these books and supplements and they have remained part of the Orthodox and Catholic Bibles since that time, although the two churches have different texts as part of their biblical canons.

An additional question for the early church regarding the Old Testament was whether it should be included in the Christian scriptures at all. While much of the New Testament church was Jewish and its writings often addressed matters relating to Jews becoming Christians and sharing a faith with those from a Gentile background, the church as it spread became predominantly Gentile and Greek-thinking in nature. Given that these people were not circumcised into the Abrahamic covenant and never came under the Mosaic law, there was a question concerning the authority of the Old Testament over their lives and even about whether the Old Testament spoke of the same God revealed in Jesus. The early heretic Marcion is perhaps the most famous advocate of removing the Jewish scriptures from the Christian sacred texts.

The response of the church may be helpful to correct a current trend to do with reading the Old Testament. Much of our concern today seems to be to "find Jesus" in Old Testament writings. This shows a great potential problem with our doctrine of God. Undoubtedly, there are messianic prophecies in the Old Testament that helped the church to recognize Jesus as the Christ, as the New Testament writings show. However, the Old Testament is primarily a revelation of God, in New Testament terms as Father and Holy Spirit, not a revelation of the incarnate Word – in fact, word and wisdom of God language in the Old Testament generally refers to the Spirit, not the Son.

The early church focused on the wider doctrine of God as the reason for the importance of including the Old Testament in the Christian scriptures, partly because their understanding of Christ was very incomplete at this stage (and maybe it always should be partially incomplete), and partly because the God that they understood in the Old Testament was essentially the same as that revealed in Christ and Spirit – angry at sin and yet gracious towards sinners through covenants of love. At this stage of the church's development, the focus was much more on how the Old Testament helped us understand the nature of Jesus than on how Jesus helped us understand the Old Testament: Scripture as a witness to Jesus, rather than Jesus as the sole purpose of Scripture. There is a worrying rhetoric today about Jesus being all that we need, when Scripture and the historic church would be firm in stating that we need Father, Son, and Spirit, each as they are revealed to be and with what they are revealed as doing, without confusing the identity or work of any of the three.

Beyond these concepts of God, the early Christian leaders were convinced of the need to retain the Old Testament in its entirety as the basis for the Christian faith that was developing in its understanding and, as we will shortly see, as it began to build its own written tradition. The early church used the revelation of the Old Testament as an important tool in the interpretation of the new revelations of God in Christ, the Spirit of Christ, and the church.

New Testament

Some of the New Testament writings were gaining authority for the church even in their own times – 2 Peter 3:16 indicates that Paul's writings were already considered scriptural when this letter was written. The four Gospels likewise seem to have been widely accepted as sources for the life of Jesus. There has been a lengthy discussion about the existence of another document, normally called simply "Q", which is primarily thought to comprise a set of Jesus' sayings that may be the basis for different emphases and stories in the first three Gospels, which otherwise largely overlap with each other. Whether or not this existed, there was certainly a strong oral tradition about Jesus, which would have included events in his life and his teachings, in the apostolic and post-apostolic period.

Beyond these books, there are a range of texts that were used by the early church with varying degrees of authority, some of which were collected into versions of what would become the New Testament. Of the books that were ultimately included, Hebrews, 2 Peter, Revelation, 2 and 3 John, James, and Jude were all undecided on at some point – the New Testament used by Origen in the mid-third century contained only Revelation of all these books. Other works were used by the church for their teaching on faith and practice although they were not finally included: the letter of Clement to Rome, the *Didache* (or Writings of the Twelve), the Shepherd of Hermas, and the Revelation to Peter, among others.

What was most important for the early church was not precisely which written texts they were reading but the faith that they held and were living out. A good example of this is Ignatius of Antioch, one of a group known as the Apostolic Fathers, who wrote a series of letters to churches sometime around AD 100. These were therefore written well after the first three Gospels and Paul's letters, yet Ignatius does not quote from these texts to back up his teachings, although he does occasionally use phrases that occurred in earlier writings – this of course was the time when the last of the eyewitnesses to events recorded in the New Testament were still alive. The emphasis is on the faith of the church and a desire that the congregations should listen to their leaders rather than to any travelling teachers who might teach a more attractive gospel but not one in line with that received from the apostles.

The writings that would form the New Testament were important as witnesses to the faith of the church, rather than being simply an authority in themselves. The main reason for this was that those who were deemed to be teaching incorrectly were generally working with the same texts – few people try to be heretics or have this as their life goal. One of the most famous examples of this would again be Arius, who denied the full divinity of Christ because he was said to be the Son of God. Arius was grounding his theology in the scriptures and it took a great deal of work by the church, seeking the true faith that had been passed down, for his ideas to be countered well.

When trying to explain the Christian position, concepts borrowed from Greek philosophy were often used to process the revelation in the Bible and form an argument. The idea of the Son being "of one being" with the Father (*homoousios*) that was presented in the Nicene Creed to respond to Arius uses Aristotle's ideas of being rather than something found in the Bible – in this context, interestingly, Philippians 2:6 ("who being in very nature God" in my NIV) actually uses the Greek word for "shape" or "outward expression" (*morphe*) rather than any idea of innate nature. It was as the church and its key thinkers sought to protect members from teaching deemed incorrect that they used tools both linguistic and philosophical from their society to establish sound doctrines for people to follow.

As we have seen, the emphasis for the early church was consistently on the faith held and expressed by believers, and it was this that the nature of both church and Scripture was to support. The church increasingly focused on these texts rather than the hundreds of others that were around from the early decades because they were reliable witnesses to the faith that was proclaimed, although even these needed to be read with correct guidance to avoid corruptions coming into the faith.

From our modern perspective, it is easy to picture our own experience reflected in the early church, as if each family had a copy of the Bible to read. A little consideration is enough to remind us that in those days, long before the printing press and with literacy rates far lower than today, access to the written word was a corporate experience that for a long time would only involve copies that had been made of certain parts of what would become the New Testament.

INTERPRETATION

There is a great concentration in many churches on the "sound" interpretation of Scripture – something that should be well supported. One question that will always be discussed in relation to this is: how do we define a sound interpretation of Scripture?[7] At the outset we need to recognize that there are difficulties both proposed and contained in the Bible itself. The use of Old Testament passages by New Testament writers would not pass most modern hermeneutical (interpretation) tests, with the context and original audience often not borne in mind when verses are quoted by New Testament writers. In addition, in the verse referred to above from 2 Peter, there is a recognition that Paul's letters "contain some things that are hard to understand, which ignorant and unstable people distort, as they do the other Scriptures, to their own destruction" (2 Peter 3:16).

With the New Testament gradually gaining authority in the early decades of the church and only being finalized much later, it is slightly difficult to pinpoint the earliest methods of interpretation. From the end of the first century we do start to have some language repeated, most notably in the letters of Ignatius of Antioch, but these are simply possible references rather than sermons or commentaries on passages – the original author and context are not discussed.

---

7   For some readers, the idea of the "perspicacity of Scripture" will leap to mind at this point. We will look at that idea when we get to the Reformation section of this chapter.

As regards the use of the Old Testament, we have an important early example from Christian writings showing a rather free interpretive approach in the epistle of Barnabas, one of a collection of writings known as the Apostolic Fathers. This letter, not written by Barnabas the companion of Paul but probably around AD 100, was important for the early church and was still being considered for inclusion in the New Testament canon into the third century. The teaching of the Christian faith contained in the work is orthodox, with the Old Testament scriptures used as an authority for points the writer is making. There is a lengthy section reinterpreting the food rules in the Mosaic law, indicating that they were never intended literally, but figuratively: the law against eating pork is said to encourage people not to consort with people who are like pigs; the law against eating hyenas was to discourage fornication because hyenas were believed to be hermaphrodites. It seems a rather free approach to interpretation, to say the least.

With what becomes the New Testament, there is a progression of interaction by writers with these books. By the early years of the second century, certain texts – the first three Gospels and some of the Pauline letters – begin to be referred to briefly as authorities in Christian writing, indicating that they are widely known and accepted. By the end of the second century, we can see in the work of people such as Irenaeus of Lyon and Tertullian of Carthage an appeal to a wider set of books as authorities for the faith, although at this stage the texts are used as support for the teaching of the faith rather than in what might be termed a commentary or exegesis.[8] The first writer to produce what can be recognized as commentaries was Origen of Alexandria in the third century, and by the end

---

8 It is worth noting that Irenaeus appeals to *The Shepherd of Hermas* as scriptural, indicating that the written authorities for the Christian faith were still not decided.

of that century the New Testament books were being used much more systematically to support Christian teaching.

From this point on, the role of Scripture is crucial in forming Christian thought, with commentaries being produced and texts of sermons being distributed – most famously those of John Chrysostom, a writer admired for the way in which he communicated the faith. However, the role of Scripture is still not above that of the faith of the church to which it bears witness, and the church seeks to protect a right use and interpretation of the New Testament.

The example of Arius, whom we have already mentioned, is a good one in this regard. Of the titles given to Jesus Christ in the Bible, "Son of God" is one of the most frequently applied by a variety of New Testament writers. The bare meaning of this term would seem to lean more towards Arius's idea that Jesus originated in the Father and thus had a beginning, before the creation of this world. But the faith of the church argued against such an interpretation, and therefore there was a need to clarify how we should understand Jesus as the Son of God. The creeds that were published by the church in the fourth century emphasized that Jesus was "begotten, not made", seeking to avoid the concept of creation that would indicate a beginning for the being of Christ.

Beyond this desire to ensure that Scripture is interpreted in line with the faith maintained by the church, two schools of thought have been discerned that indicate two broad approaches to interpreting the Bible, and to certain areas of Christian thought. These are termed "Alexandrian" and "Antiochene", depending on which of these significant Christian centres the major writers were more associated with. There were no actual schools, and the writers grouped together under each of these names were only loosely united in their method and thought, but when it comes to reading Scripture the distinction is a useful generalization.

The Antiochene writers focused more on a literal reading of the Bible, looking directly at what is stated in the text as the basis for our knowledge of who God is and what he does. The Alexandrians favoured wider interpretations of passages, believing that God is fundamentally incomprehensible and thus that any words used are only the initial stage of an approach towards who God actually is. In reality, very few writers exclusively used either one or the other of these methods as they taught, defended, and discussed various aspects of the Christian faith.

The Legacy

The early centuries when Christians were seeking to understand and express well the faith as it was passed on from Christ and the apostles, with Scripture as an increasingly important witness, are known as the Patristic Period, or the time of the Church Fathers. Throughout this time, beliefs were captured on most of the central aspects of Christianity; beliefs that remain vital to the church today. Some of these were clearly stated in the Bible, such as the virgin birth of Christ and the resurrection; others required great additional and careful work to grasp and to communicate, such as the nature of the godhead and the union of human and divine in Christ.

The different histories and methods of the Western and Eastern Roman empires took the heritage from the Patristic Period down different routes. In the East, the Roman empire survived for a thousand years past the West, finally falling in 1453. This meant that there was little disruption to the church in respect of its organization, its approach to theology, or its membership. With a greater role for the mystical and a more open philosophical approach, the teaching of the Eastern Church was founded on the agreed theology contained in the creeds published by the whole church, but beyond this there was little that was absolutely fixed. Rather, there was an openness to theological discussion that did not demand or even seek the final answer to which more systematic Western theology tended. Scripture and the core faith of the church were intertwined for the Orthodox Churches, with the latter involving a right belief in a fairly small set of doctrines.

The disruption to the Western Church soon after the time of Augustine, caused by the fall of the Western Roman empire, was touched on in the previous chapter. What did this mean for the development of the approach to Scripture? Western Europe fell into the "Dark Ages", a disputable term but one that does reflect a period of around 600 years when there was less significant writing, particularly in theology and philosophy. It was not completely barren, but the scholarly work that was done was generally more about preserving the teaching of the church than adding to it.

The result was that, whereas there was a continued dynamism in the study of Christianity in the East, with writers such as John of Damascus and Photius, things settled into rather a solid state in the West, with the authority of the Scriptures and their right interpretation found in the writings of the Fathers, particularly Augustine as the major Latin writer, and the creeds. Once education and study restarted in earnest from the twelfth century onwards, the faith upheld by this unity of Scripture and tradition was unquestionable – as was shown in the earlier note on Peter Abelard's *Sic et Non*.

The more logical, less mystical approach to thought and belief in the West led to a more structured approach both to theology and to the reading of Scripture to protect the faith of the church's members. Soon after the fall of the Western Roman empire, an additional factor that affected this area was the drop in literacy rates, which meant that only certain people in a society could read the Bible. A pathway to literacy and study of the Bible was soon available in the monastic movement that developed from St Benedict, which at its beginnings and for most of its history was available to all baptized believers willing and able to commit themselves to that life.

For several centuries, however, reading the Bible was confined to the few by the societal situation, and centuries of practice inevitably conditioned people and institutions. The transition that the church made as society shifted away from the more educated Roman empire had many strong points. There was a good pastoral emphasis, seen most clearly in the writings of Pope Gregory the Great, while the faith was communicated not only through the catechism and the liturgy but also through architecture and art. There was an expectation of divine action that can be seen in the accounts of the miraculous that dominate the stories of the church during this period – Bede's account of the English experience is packed full of God's action in and through the church. The mission of the church to unreached peoples was a high priority, first in the reconversion of the English kingdoms and then through the conversion of Germany and Scandinavia. The transition to being church and communicating the core faith was generally well made in the loss of Roman civilization, but the reverse transition that was needed from the twelfth century onwards, as European society developed through the Renaissance and the increase in education and urbanization, was far less effective.

THE MEDIEVAL PERIOD

Things changed significantly for the church from the end of the eleventh century, with Anselm of Canterbury bringing a new approach to the Christian faith in the use of reason to explore and build on the teaching received from Scripture and the Church Fathers. This quickly led to a reaction by way of a development in the mystical tradition that took a different approach to the Christian life and experience. Both of these were more influential in the "higher" levels of the medieval church, in the monasteries and the universities, and only partly dripped down into the public consciousness. There we see a growing dissatisfaction with aspects of the church's approach to Scripture, and all of these elements played a part in the reforming efforts of the sixteenth century.

Faith Seeking Understanding

The phrase "Faith Seeking Understanding" comes from Augustine's reading of Isaiah, but was popularized by Anselm, who ushered in a movement known as scholasticism, in which reason is applied to the faith of the church. Anselm himself is an interesting study since, in a surface reading, many of his books seem to be simply expressions of human reason with little or no reference to either the Bible or the writings of the Church Fathers. But such an impression misunderstands Anselm's project, which is founded on an acceptance of the authority of the church and seeks to explore God, life, and the world from this basis using the reason God has given him. An example of this would be his Ontological Argument, which presupposes the existence of God, or his exploration of the being of God that ends with the Trinity as presented by Augustine despite never referring to Augustine's work.

For Anselm, therefore, both Scripture and its interpretation by the church are accepted and unquestionable pillars on which he can build and which will always guide and be the end point of his discussions. The deeper discussions of faith that begin and develop make use of other sources of the revelation of God: in creation; in humans made in the (albeit tarnished) image of God, particularly in elements of rationality and creativity that reflect the being of God; in the church's experiences where the Spirit is active.

At this initial stage of the medieval theological project, the relationship between faith and reason is clear, with the former established and unquestionable. Fairly soon after this the roles of faith and reason begin to shift, with the earliest noticeable evidence being Peter Abelard highlighting contrasts present in the teaching of the Church Fathers. The most important work for the medieval period was written by a man named Peter Lombard, whose *Sentences* became the textbook for the study of the Christian faith for many centuries. This is more systematic and comprehensive than the works of Anselm, which tend to be individual studies of aspects of theology, but it generally follows his method of establishing the faith and defending and explaining it through the use of reason.

By the time of Thomas Aquinas in the thirteenth century, theology and philosophy had become closely interwoven as subjects of study. Aquinas is known for his use of Aristotle both in method and in the principles that he uses to discuss various aspects of his thought. It is noticeable when reading Aquinas that, in areas not clearly found in the Bible, Aristotle is accepted as an authority independent of explicit scriptural teaching. An early example of this, in his great work the *Summa Theologia*, is on the relationship between goodness and being, where the statement of Aquinas's position only contains a quotation from Aristotle's *Ethics*.

In Aquinas's work, where specific Christian issues are discussed – such as salvation by grace – the references are dominated by Scripture and the Church Fathers; in areas that are less gospel-focused, Aristotle also has a voice intended to help the reader understand the teaching. What we see as this scholastic movement develops is a changing role of Scripture, from the stable foundation (together with its right interpretation) to a key authority but with other authorities recognized in method, in principles of thought, and in content.

It is important to look in a little depth at Aquinas because his work, and what builds on it, becomes an important area of critique for many Protestant reformers, while the Catholic Reformation tends more toward Aquinas's teaching than to that of Augustine or Peter Lombard – the other two most senior names in the history of theology. In the years between Aquinas and the Reformation, there is a move away from the level of integration of theology with philosophy that we see in Aquinas's work (although this was a gradual and uneven process). In many places and in the work of writers we see the two being studied separately and in different ways: philosophy was more empirical, testing hypotheses on the basis of the evidence available; theology was more fideistic (faith-based), holding to the faith as an unquestioned authority and discussing issues only after recognizing this basis.

By the sixteenth century, there was a concern about the role of Scripture in all this theological discussion, with the tools for interpretation seemingly becoming dominant over the text itself, with the result that elements of the Bible's teachings –

some central to the Christian gospel – seemed to be hidden if not lost in much that was written or taught. There was a need to reclaim Scripture's authority for the teaching of the church.

Faith Seeking Experience

This is not a historical phrase, as Anselm's "Faith Seeking Understanding" was, but it serves well to describe a second trend in the use of Scripture in the medieval church: what may be termed the mystical tradition. Where the scholastics took the Bible and the faith as the unquestioned basis for their rational explorations of the being, revelation, and action of God, the mystics sought from the same foundation to experience God in prayer and to consider what this meant for the life of the church.

There had always been a mystical element to the Christian church because the gospel is ultimately mysterious. Paul uses the word "mystery" sixteen times in his letters, sometimes linked to an understanding through Christ or his own teaching, but also as something that remains a mystery even in the time of the church; hence salvation is by faith, not by understanding. This continued in the early church, shown in relation to the Bible by the fact that writers took a more allegorical approach to Scripture at times rather than focusing solely on the literal meaning.

One of the most important formative thinkers in the mystical tradition is known as Dionysius the Areopagite or Pseudo-Dionysius (I don't make these names up, but I suppose it gives us more options for children's names taken from Christian history). This was an unknown writer, probably from Syria around AD 500, writing under the name of one of Paul's converts in Athens, a fact that lent his work great authority in the church through the medieval period. The method behind his thought is known as "Apophatic theology", which seeks a higher view of God by recognizing what God is not. In this approach to God, Scripture becomes the first phase of a Christian's experience of God in establishing truths about his nature and action as revealed in ways that we can understand – through language and stories. The fullness of God's being must, however, be beyond what any human language can communicate; so by saying "God is love", we both utter a truth as revealed in Scripture and yet also limit God if we believe that the love God is can be fully comprehended through any ideas or experiences in our understanding in this world.

Whereas the scholastic movement sought to move from Scripture and tradition to explain the faith more fully, the mystical movement held that the purpose of God's revelation was an experience of God. In the medieval period, there was a quick reaction against the development of theology, the study of God, headed by Bernard of Clairvaux, who thought the idea ridiculous: who were humans to study God? Our role was surely to experience and worship him.

This did not mean switching off the mind – Bernard wrote some wonderful reflections on God – but that the human mind should be subject to the revelation of God, which included Scripture, tradition, and experience. Bernard worked heavily with Scripture, but did not exclusively follow either a literal or an allegorical reading. His most famous work on the Bible, a set of eighty-six sermons on the Song of Songs, takes the allegorical approach that this biblical book is not about human sexuality but is a picture of God's love in his very being and for his church. It is interesting, given John Calvin's renown for his *Institutes of the Christian Religion*, quite a systematic work on the Christian faith, that one of the writers he drew on extensively in his own writing was Bernard of Clairvaux.

The mystical tradition continued to be strong throughout the medieval period, as seen in writers such as Julian of Norwich, Walter Hilton, and Johann Eckhart. The sixteenth century proved to be a particularly rich period for Christian mysticism, with Teresa of Avila (who wrote *The Interior Castle*), St John of the Cross (*The Dark Night of the Soul*) and Ignatius Loyola (*The Spiritual Exercises*) all living and working at this time.

There is one other element of the mystical side of Christianity that needs to be mentioned here, and that is the church's teaching on the sacraments. This comes, via the Latin *sacer* ("sacred, holy"), from the Greek *Mysterion*, meaning "mystery", and maintains that one of the central connections between God and humankind comes through these instruments of grace as indicated by Scripture and then developed by the church into an essential part of the faith experience.

Two of what would become the seven sacraments of the Catholic Church are clearly taught in Scripture and become vital parts of the Christian life at a very early time – baptism and Eucharist (or the Lord's Supper). The others (penance, Holy Orders, anointing the sick, confirmation, and marriage) are gradually adopted as sacraments from a basis in early church practice and then through reflection on Scripture and the faith. In the medieval period, the sacraments come under extensive scrutiny from the rational scholastics, and much of the mystery that was at their roots is removed. This is perhaps most clear in the case of penance, where the devotion that was present in the early church morphs into an almost mathematical, at times financial, approach that Luther was so critical of in the 95 Theses.

Reading the Bible

There is much to be admired in both of these traditions, as they sought to understand the revelation of God in all its forms and to obtain the greatest experience of God, but there was also a danger in each that their basis in the authority of Scripture and the faith of the church would get lost as the thought/experience became more exalted, possibly losing any connection with the roots that inspired them. An additional problem was that less able people often had to communicate the faith to the Christians in the churches because the most able thinkers and writers were generally bound for either monasteries or universities, where they were able to devote themselves most fully to their pursuits.

The situation was not helped by secular appointments to ecclesial positions – think Henry II appointing his friend Thomas Becket to be Archbishop of Canterbury when he had no training for or experience of leading the church. The result of all this was often not a positive experience for those lay Christians who wanted a robust, or even adequate, understanding of their faith. This would be a growing problem through the medieval period as literacy rates rose from the end of the eleventh century, and when this was put together with growing towns and cities where ideas could be discussed, the simpler presentation of the faith that had been effective during the harsher centuries following the break-up of the Roman empire became increasingly insufficient for the developing critical congregations of Europe.

The most prominent voice calling the church back to the authority of the Bible in the medieval period was that of John Wycliffe. His focal point was opposing the ability of the church and the pope to define the faith without recognizing the authority of Scripture over them, which he expressed most clearly in his work *On the Truth of Holy Scripture*. Wycliffe is famously known in connection with a translation of the Bible to make it available in the native language (the vernacular) during the late fourteenth century. Scholars are generally agreed that Wycliffe himself was not the main translator – if he was involved at all – but more the inspiration for this project. As this occurred before the invention of the printing press, it was not widely available despite clearly having some popularity (most of the remaining copies are only parts of the Bible rather than complete translations).

The church reacted swiftly to condemn this project, formally in the *Constitutions* published in 1409 regarding the preaching and translation of the Bible. It is important to recognize that this was not a blanket ban on anyone reading the Bible in English – many parts had been published in translation, with commentaries to guide the reader – but an attempt to counter a challenge to the authority of the church and to protect people's faith. As we have seen, the faith that was communicated was of paramount importance in the context of the early struggles against various heresies, and there was a fear that opening the Bible up for anyone to read and decide what it meant was dangerous. Wycliffe himself would have been against this kind of radical approach, believing that it should be read alongside the church.

The condemnation of Wycliffe and his followers, soon followed on the continent by the trial and execution of Jan Hus who had likewise attacked the teaching of the church and the pope, demonstrated, however, that this was not just a matter of the protection of faith but also one of unquestionable authority. In Renaissance Europe, with a growing humanism that sought wisdom from different sources, with increasing knowledge of biblical languages that allowed for critique of the Latin translation of the Bible, and with the invention of the printing press in the middle of the fifteenth century, such an absolute authoritarian stance was ripe for challenge.

Conclusion

All three of these elements were involved in the Reformation writings on the Bible, although the mystical point was more specifically applied to the sacraments than to the wider method. On the sacraments, the reformers debated even the two some retained – baptism and the Lord's Supper – from the perspective of Scripture, while the Catholic Reformation upheld all seven on the grounds that they were based on scriptural teaching and principles.

The scholastic approach was attacked fiercely by the reformers for its effect in extending elements of church faith and practice beyond or away from the teaching of the Bible. The spread of the Protestant groups was enabled by the fact that there was a tradition present with popular support that critiqued the absolute authority of church and pope, with the Bible a key element in voices challenging the current situation.

REFORMATION VIEWS

We will look at five approaches to Scripture from reforming movements in the first half of the sixteenth century, seeking to clarify the role of the Bible in the faith of the church. What is particularly noticeable when reading through the writings of the major reformers is the nuanced differences in their approach to Scripture and some of the results of this in their theology and discussions. Rather than being a unifying feature, it was this root method that caused many of the disagreements between Protestant groups, and was at the centre of many of their critiques of the Catholic Church.

Martin Luther

Luther is a complex person to understand in relation to his view of Scripture, partly because of his own work on the Bible in his context, but mostly because of the nature of his attacks on others for their misuse of it. We will begin with what we can see in his more constructive works, helping people to read the Bible and concerning the role that it should play in the reform of the church, before examining four groups or individuals with whom he disagreed over how they used Scripture.

The obvious starting point is Luther's own translation of the Bible. This began while he was staying in the Wartburg, a castle that he was taken to for his own protection, where he produced a mass of writing. In this first stage Luther completed the translation of the New Testament into German, with the Old Testament coming later, a project that has had profound effects on the German language ever since.

In the light of our look at the early church and Scripture, it is important to recognize that Luther altered the canon of the Old and New Testaments that had been recognized in the earlier Council of Chalcedon and used for the previous thousand years, removing the books that comprise the Apocrypha from their standard positions in the Old Testament and inserting them between the Old and New Testaments (with a later note that these texts were not equal to the Scriptures, but useful for Christians). In like manner, Luther took certain books from their usual places in the New Testament, notably James and

Hebrews, and moved them to the end (because of theological issues rather than because they were disputable documents in the early church). With regard to the concept of Scripture, these are important factors, given that there is nothing integral to the Bible to indicate which texts should be included in the final Christian Bible. We must recognize in this that Luther was taking upon himself an authority to revise how readers engaged with certain portions of what could be considered Scripture.

There are strong echoes in Luther's work of Wycliffe's project 150 years earlier: putting the Bible into the hands of the people, away from the control of the church. We must remember that translations were not new even in Wycliffe's time, but had previously always been accompanied by commentaries that sought to fix the meaning and application of passages. Luther's Bible does allow a degree of freedom, although we need to recognize that, in contrast to Wycliffe, Luther also published prefaces on each of the books of the Bible as well as lectures or sermons that prepared someone for and to some extent guided the reading of books. This was particularly true in Luther's great speciality, the book of Romans, where the preface is so extensive that it becomes a minor commentary, while his lectures on Romans were also published.[9]

It was important for Luther that the Bible be more easily available to show the wider church how reform was, as he believed, desperately needed in some areas to return to a true faith. He was concerned that two forces in particular were corrupting the church: the papacy with a worldly agenda, and the scholastics with a dependence on human reason and therefore human worth. Both lacked the humble attitude to

---

9   Regarding Romans, it is also worth noting that Luther inserted a word into his translation of Romans 3:28 so that it reads as justification by faith *alone*. Luther's defence was that this was necessary to translate the Greek sense into the German language, but debates will always continue on this point. It is worth noting that Luther was not the first to include this concept in a copy of Romans.

Scripture that Luther desired, while the protest that developed in the years immediately after the publication of the 95 Theses led to two further objects of attack in other reforming groups who in different ways, in his opinion, lacked humility before the word of God.

Luther's realization from the book of Romans that a person is justified by faith alone was a core element in the construction of his 95 Theses, and a first glance through these shows that much of the theology he was moving towards retained strong Catholic elements. In his *Exposition of the Theses*, Luther included a letter to the pope, Leo X, about his purpose in putting forward this document for the church's consideration, in which he showed at this point a continuing acknowledgment of the authority of the papacy:

> *In them all may see, who will, how purely and simply I have sought after and cherished the power of Church and reverence for the keys. … Wherefore, most blessed Father, I cast myself at the feet of your Holiness, with all that I have and all that I am. Quicken, kill, call, recall, approve, reprove, as you will. In your voice I shall recognize the voice of Christ directing you and speaking in you.*[10]

This recognition of papal authority did not last long, as it became clear to Luther that the false teaching and practice he perceived in the commercial approach of the church to grace not only affected priests and bishops, but were aspects that the highest ranks of the papacy were unwilling to reform on the basis of his discoveries in the Bible. This clarifies the role of Scripture in Luther's writing, no longer simply as something

---

10   Letter to Leo X in the preface to Luther's *Explanation of the 95 Theses*.

that is brought to the church to consider how it affects faith and practice, but as the rule that the church, even the pope, must submit to.

Even in this later position, we must always remember Luther's desire to reform the church rather than to restart it, with the importance of the heritage of interpretation – particularly that of Augustine, but also of other writers who duly revered the faith communicated in the Bible – continuing to be shown in many areas of Luther's thought. Two of these that demonstrate the point are his teachings on Mary and on purgatory. In both of these Luther does not simply toe the line in following the predominant Catholic teaching of his day, but his views on Scripture lead him rather to seek reform than to deny what is being taught. Regarding Mary, Luther is in line with other reformers in retaining a belief in her perpetual virginity, while he writes on many occasions of her sinlessness – albeit in this he seems to change from a belief about this beginning at her conception (a position more radical than that taught by Aquinas) to a complete purity that begins at Christ's conception. Luther retained a belief in some form of purgatory throughout his life, extensively reforming the Catholic Church's beliefs and practices associated with this, but following Augustine's, whereas Calvin later would disagree with Augustine.

In respect of the church and Scripture, therefore, Luther wished ultimately to subject the authority of the church to the authority of the Bible; with the scholastics there was a slightly different task in subjecting human reason to the Bible. The most notable battle that Luther fought on this front was with Desiderius Erasmus, the great humanist philosopher and theologian, over the freedom of the human will. Erasmus taught that the human will has an important part to play even in salvation, and Luther's argument against this centres on the approach to the Bible. Erasmus does reluctantly accept the authority of the Bible and the church, yet states that many areas in the Bible are unclear. Against this, Luther acknowledges that there may be words or phrases that are obscure, yet the wider message of the gospel and the nature of humanity is clear:

> *All the things, therefore, contained in the scriptures*
> *are made clear, although some places, because the*
> *words are not understood, are still obscure. But*
> *to know that all things in the scriptures are set in*
> *the clearest light, and then, because a few words*
> *are obscure, to report that the things are obscure,*
> *is absurd and impious. If the words are obscure*
> *in one place, yet they are clear in another. But,*
> *however, the same thing that has been most openly*
> *declared to the whole world is both spoken of in the*
> *scriptures in plain words, and also still lies hidden*
> *in obscure words.*[11]

Luther sees the project of theology in the universities being overtaken in the early sixteenth century by the perceived wisdom of humanity, creating complications in the teaching of Christianity that are unnecessary if one simply upholds the authority of the Bible. The cause, as is indicated in his critique of Erasmus, seems to be only partly a desire for great philosophical consideration, but is also because parts of the Bible's teachings are unattractive for a society that is increasingly stressing the development of humankind and in this reducing its reliance on God.

In these ongoing challenges to the existing church, Luther

---

11 Luther, *Bondage of the Will*, section 3.

plays a crucial role in allowing others to seek reforms using their own methods. The success of Luther's Reformation (in that it changed the church in Wittenberg rather than because it was an ideal reformation) created the conditions for other places and people to remove themselves from the church's authority and teaching. However, as we shall see, Luther was quick to condemn those he thought had not rightly grasped the basis for any reformation in the authority of Scripture.

Ulrich Zwingli

Zwingli's path towards reforming the church was rather different from Luther's. Where Luther was embedded in the life and thought of the church as a monk and a university lecturer, realizing truths of the gospel from Scripture and recognizing a need for reform, Zwingli took a more critical approach earlier in his life and ministry. Influenced by a humanist education and educated in Greek to read the New Testament directly, Zwingli began to teach in church directly from the Bible rather than processing biblical texts through an understood interpretation.

This resulted in a more radical approach to church teaching than that adopted by Martin Luther, with Zwingli far more removed from the traditional teaching of the church. Whereas Luther had grown through his life and studies to acquire such a devotion to the church that his revelations shocked him into seeking major reforms, Zwingli's education had included stronger humanist elements from the beginning and this involved a more critical outlook on all aspects of life, including religion.

In the Swiss context, where the influence of the church in worldly affairs had been great, and a factor in the Swiss reformations was the liberation of all aspects of society from church control, there was less of a sense of seeking to discern areas in the current situation that might need reforming and more of a belief that a major overhaul was required. Zwingli's studies confirmed him in this opinion and much that seemed mere superstition was challenged, along with any aspect of Christian teaching that sought to trust in the wisdom of people rather than God.

Early in his career Zwingli was notable for his use of Scripture in sermons, particularly the raw way in which he engaged with biblical texts without the surrounding tradition. Following the break from the Catholic Church in Zurich, he naturally became a leading figure and engaged successfully in debates with Catholics using his method of arguing directly from the Bible. Zwingli led Zurich through a series of reforms in the early 1520s, culminating in the abolition of the Mass in 1525.

Zwingli's method led to two battles with other reformers. The first was with Luther, with whom Zwingli famously disagreed over what happened during the Lord's Supper. Luther rejected transubstantiation, but, based on the words of Christ, "This is my body", held to a real presence of Christ in the bread and wine. Zwingli wanted a more radical break from the church in this area and, utilizing some linguistic tools from fellow humanists, reinterpreted the "is" to mean "symbolizes", thereby denying any bodily presence of Christ. In this case, Zwingli was criticized by fellow reformers for not following the bare meaning of the text in his proposed theology.

In the second instance, Zwingli was seen to hold on too tightly to a traditional theology. Here, his opponents were Anabaptists in Zurich who, favouring a return to the authority of Scripture, argued that there was no explicit baptism of infants in the New Testament and so the practice should be ended. Zwingli engaged in debate with these too, seeking to show from cases of household baptism, from the relation of baptism to circumcision, and from Paul's teaching on Christian families that infant baptism should be retained. But the Anabaptists claimed that such a view contradicted his insistence on the absolute authority of the Bible. It should be noted here that Catholic opponents of Zwingli rather revelled in the fact that his own reformation was being challenged on the very grounds on which he sought to distance himself from the Catholic Church.

Zwingli's approach was therefore more radically reforming than Luther's in his idea of Scripture being set above tradition, but he certainly did not encourage a free, uncritical reading of the Bible because of the potential danger that such a subjective method might lead to a misreading of key elements of biblical teaching.

Radical reformation

The Anabaptists in Zurich were one incarnation of a more radical reforming movement that was present around Europe in a variety of forms with little unity, although many were lumped together under the loose term "Anabaptist" because of the common denial of infant baptism. This, though, was rarely the focus of the differences between them and both the Catholic Church and other protesting voices, since the departure on the doctrine of baptism resulted from deeper-seated differences in ideas about the church and the Bible.

We have relatively little that survives directly from early Anabaptist leaders, mostly because of the opposition of all other groups and the resulting persecution that they suffered (see Introduction). As a result, Menno Simons has become an important lens (along with the Schleitheim Confession) through which we have access to the Anabaptists, although it is clear historically that he was not a prime leader – rather, his work suffered from members leaving to join more radical Anabaptist groups. Simons himself had little interaction with other major reformers, largely because the development of his thought was gradual, reaching its maturity only in the mid-1530s.

We have already seen that the so-called "Zwickau prophets" became popular owing to their stand against the religiosity of Catholicism and their advocacy of a much greater attention to the Spirit. Three of their leaders were expelled from Zwickau for this and later went to Wittenberg to teach that the sole authority in faith should be the Spirit of God, who had no connection to either Christ or the Bible. The presence of these men in Wittenberg itself during Luther's absence in the Wartburg made them prime exemplars of many of the teachings of radical groups more widely.

It is impossible to tell how far Andreas von Karlstadt, the leader of the Reformation in Wittenberg during Luther's absence, was affected by the teachings of the Zwickau prophets. His initial distance from Luther centred on the Lord's Supper and his quest for moral perfection in the Christian life, but Karlstadt did develop Anabaptist views and this became an additional factor in his condemnation by Luther. More clear were the effects of Zwickau on Thomas Müntzer, whose views were sometimes cited by Luther as "fanatical", and against such men Luther wrote a lengthy treatise, *Against the Heavenly Prophets*. He also referred to such views in the Smalcald Articles of 1537, where he stated that men such as Karlstadt and Müntzer had elevated their experience of the Spirit above the Bible, with Müntzer calling Luther and his like "learned in Scripture" whereas Müntzer himself was "learned in the

Spirit". Luther compared such a view to that of the papacy in taking control of the faith, stating that the Spirit continues to communicate in line with the revelation of Scripture, which means that we cannot seek to divorce our experience of the Spirit from the reading of the word of God.

The general view of the Anabaptists is reflected in some of Calvin's statements about them in his *Institutes of the Christian Religion*. Calvin had had some contact with part of the movement when he was involved in the prosecution of Servetus in Geneva for heresy. Calvin writes, in the context of the old and new covenants in Scripture working together, that his argument about the "inherent efficacy" of the Bible to communicate the gospel to the sober believer would seem "futile and almost ridiculous to the supercilious Anabaptists". It would seem that more moderate voices in the wider Anabaptist body, such as that of Menno Simons, did not come through strongly in perceptions of the movement, despite his closer adherence to Scripture as the authority for his teaching.

John Calvin

Forming his theology a generation later than the first Protestant voices and aided by a well-trained, logical mind, Calvin was separated to some extent from Luther's first, inspired challenge to the church, from Zwingli's humanist roots, and from the spiritual fervour of the Anabaptists. Not that any of these elements were entirely lacking from Calvin's life and thought, but he was able by nature and circumstance to take a somewhat more considered view and this can best be seen in the thorough, systematic approach of the *Institutes*.

Calvin addresses the essential role of Scripture in the Christian faith very early in book one of the *Institutes* after acknowledging a revelation of God in creation. He states that the fallen nature of humankind makes it essential that there is this special revelation of God, to which we must first be obedient in order for our faith to be made complete. This is a first stage in Calvin's encouragement to his readers to be humble before Scripture, something that permeates all his considerations of the role of the Bible.

Calvin's ideas on Scripture are closely entwined with his initial thought on the Holy Spirit, and the role of the Spirit is not only that of inspiring the biblical writers, but also includes the teaching of the meaning of Scripture to believers and the confirmation of this in the experience of Christians. In this second point, Calvin does not limit the witness to the Bible's authority solely to texts from the Bible, but upholds the testimony of the church through the centuries and has a particular regard for the martyrs, who, through assurance from the Spirit that they had a true faith from Scripture, were able to face death with confidence.

There are three groups against whose use of the Bible Calvin explicitly writes; their positions differ in some respects but they are united in their desire to place themselves in some way above the Bible as authorities. The first is clearly the Catholic Church in its institutional guise, which in Calvin's view has in many areas of theology extended the beliefs called for far beyond and even away from the teaching of the Bible. The role of tradition is important in this, and Calvin is certainly not against that in understanding the faith of the church in the Bible. Reading Calvin's work, one is impressed by his vast knowledge of thinkers throughout the history of the church and his appeal to a very wide range in support of his teaching. It is rare for Calvin to discuss any aspect of the Christian faith purely from the Bible; he also brings in historical voices to help his readers understand and gain confidence in their beliefs. The faith Calvin communicates is thus clearly the Christian faith held through the centuries, but that faith rests on the primary and absolute authority of Scripture.

The writings of the church therefore only have authority to the extent that they are in line with the Bible and they must be subjected to consideration in this regard. This applies to the creeds written by the church in the early centuries, which Calvin upholds because he believes that they convey Christian teaching correctly – there is extensive use of the Apostles' Creed in determining the structure of the *Institutes*. Like most of the major Protestant reformers, Calvin uses Augustine's theology extensively to challenge the Catholic Church, but Calvin is ready to highlight where he sees Augustine departing from biblical doctrine, most notably over the concept of purgatory. The danger he sees in the Catholic approach is that of placing the church's teaching above the Bible.

The second group, dealt with in the early chapters of the *Institutes* that look at Scripture, are the "fanatics", meaning those who would prioritize their experience of the Spirit above the authority of the Bible. We have seen some examples of this in the section on the Radical Reformation. These people appeal to the fact that they have the Spirit of Christ in them, but Calvin mocks the idea of there being any support for this without Scripture as "exceedingly ridiculous". It is not the role of the Spirit, says Calvin, to provide new revelations or doctrines, but rather to "seal on our minds the very doctrine which the gospel recommends". The danger is therefore that of prioritizing Spirit and experience over Scripture, and Calvin encourages a humble attitude in his critique of the fanatics.

The third approach that does not accord Scripture its proper authority is one that prioritizes the mind and human reason over the teaching of the Bible. This is shown in Calvin's work on free will, both in the *Institutes* and in *On the Bondage and Liberation of the Will* as he takes on the scholastics who, he believes, have relied too strongly on rational abilities and have subverted the Bible and the church's teaching on the nature of the will. For both Bible passages and historical sources, Calvin accuses his opponents of twisting and reinterpreting ideas to suit their own agenda because they are uncomfortable with what is indicated in Scripture. It is essential for Calvin that we submit to Scripture and allow the Spirit to interpret rather than imposing our own thoughts on the Bible and forcing it to say what we would like.

Catholic Reformation

The Catholic teaching on Scripture in the early sixteenth century upheld the guardianship of interpretation by the church. This is unsurprising, given the fact that it was the authority of the visible church that was at stake in much of the discussion about the Bible by protesting voices. In addition, the Catholic doctrine of the church – that it is the body of Christ inhabited by the Spirit of Christ – meant that taking the authority for the faith outside the church to anyone arguing well from the Bible would endanger the message and therefore the beliefs of those who listened.

In the early years of the Reformation, the direct challenge to the church was slow to grow. We have already seen an excerpt of a letter from Luther to Pope Leo X submitting to the authority of the papacy, and while that position did not hold for long, Luther did continue to engage with representatives of the Catholic Church in debate – the last great attempt at unifying Catholics and Lutherans in this first stage of the Reformation coming in 1541, nearly twenty-five years after the 95 Theses. Luther was adamant that he was continuing in the faith of the church through its history, making great use of Catholic writers in expressing his thought. He did not wish to leave the church, to undergo excommunication, but ultimately found no way that he could remain in the Catholic Church.

Zwingli took a more independent stance earlier than Luther, although he was also involved in debates with Catholic scholars. He seems to have had less hope of maintaining unity, but he also used teachings from the church to support his views. Some of the early Anabaptist preachers were critical of these reformers for being too much in line with the church and not stripping the faith back to the basics of the Bible. Luther and Zwingli were wary of such an approach as inviting heresy, believing that the gospel was present in the historic church but had been lost to some extent by their time.

The Catholic Church ultimately viewed the Protestant voices with the same suspicion as that with which the leading reformers viewed the radical reformers who argued for Spirit and experience above and even against Scripture. While there were debates with Luther, Zwingli, and others for many years – debating theology was a crucial part of the Catholic Church and its theological method, and the 95 Theses were probably just intended as the beginning of one such debate – once thinkers placed themselves outside the structure of the Catholic Church, there was a problem. The Spirit was seen to be assuredly active within the church, so why should a church with the Spirit submit to a critique from someone outside that church? That would seem to be placing human reason above church and Scripture, from a Catholic perspective.

This was then applied directly to the position of the Bible in the Council of Trent, the great reforming council of the Catholic Reformation:

It is in the Church that we have the Bible, that
we have the gospel and that we have authentic
understanding of the gospel, or rather, the Church
itself is the gospel, written not with ink, but by the
Spirit of the living God and not on tablets of stone,
but on tablets of flesh of the heart.

The Catholic Church would trace its experience of the use and misuse of Scripture back to the earliest church, when people wanting to challenge church teaching would repeatedly use scriptures to defend heretical positions. The battles that the church went through in that time demonstrated, according to the Catholic Church, that the Spirit would always be present to guide the thinking of the church. The development of medieval society had thrown up another bout of heresy, mostly reworked versions of earlier heresies that had been countered, and the protesting voices of the sixteenth century seemed in many ways to be simply the latest manifestation of people seeking their own truths from biblical texts outside the authority of the church.

CONCLUSION

The nature, approach to, and role of Scripture in the church were core parts of the debates around the time of the Reformation, although there is very little in any of these about individual Christians learning the faith for themselves. The leading reformers certainly encouraged people to read their Bibles, and Luther, for example, gave people the possibility with his translation, but the purpose remained a true faith in line with the church's teachings, and humility before God was the key tool that was stressed.

It is noticeable when looking at the reforming groups that there are obvious differences in their approaches to Scripture, although it is not immediately apparent whether these are contradictory, contrasting, or complementary. It seems clear that each group claims – and seems to a large degree to demonstrate – in its approach a desire to remain faithful and obedient to God in the light of the factors that have formed how it thinks about the Bible. The history of Scripture's inspiration, construction, and interpretation shows that this is not a simple matter, and maybe the church today could do with a little more humility before God, before Scripture, and before fellow members of God's church as we seek to engage with and be changed by this great revelation of God.

CHAPTER THREE

GOD'S WORK IN SALVATION: GRACE

In a study such as this, it is necessary to look at grace, faith, works, and belief, how these concepts relate to one another, and some dangers that may arise from confusing their roles in the Christian experience. There was never any doubt where to begin in dealing with these four concepts, as grace is foundational to the whole edifice of Christian thought, despite in my opinion being one of the least understood and most misapplied in practice.[12]

Grace was paramount for all those seeking to reform the church in the sixteenth century, although quite what they meant by it and how they dealt with it are often difficult to pin down. Two of the reasons for this are the way grace is used in the Bible and the way that the church had historically sought to help Christians understand its implications for their lives. A background study of these two areas is required here as, without it, one cannot appreciate many of the positions held in the sixteenth century.

---

12 Actually, there is one other factor that is vital for understanding grace – sin – but adding a fifth major theme seemed a step too far.

Let's start with a few questions that may shed light on our current understanding of grace. Because of the range of applications of grace in different church contexts, people often have a particular perspective that has been formed and solidified over time.

* How would you define grace in a single sentence?
* If grace is a gift, to what extent is it a "thing" that can be given?
* How does one receive grace?
* What areas of the Christian faith and life are tied to the concept of grace?

THE BIBLE AND THE EARLY CHURCH

When I first read Philip Yancey's book *What's So Amazing About Grace?*[13], I was a little torn about what I thought. On one level, the stories of people's experiences of grace were excellent and a great encouragement to me; and yet, in order to include all those stories, it seemed as though grace had had to be redefined each time to make the lessons fit. I had considered this to be a weakness until I started wrestling with grace and realized two things. Firstly, I had a firm yet limited concept of grace and wanted Yancey at least to nail down what he thought grace was – an unfair request, given the nature of the book. Secondly, and more fundamentally, I realized that Yancey had grasped something of the complexity and richness of grace that I had not, and the beauty of his narrative theology allowed an appreciation of this that no "What is Grace?" theology text could match.

The foundations of our understanding of grace in the Bible show the richness of the idea and the impossibility of limiting

---

13   Grand Rapids, Michigan: Zondervan, 1997.

its definition. Both the Hebrew *hesed* and the Greek *charis* are used in a plethora of ways and, given the nature of the biblical writings within specific contexts and to particular audiences, grace is consistently applied rather than theoretically discussed. A simple example would be the standard Pauline greeting in his letters: "Grace and peace to you from God our Father and the Lord Jesus Christ". What is this grace that Paul is talking about? Is he giving the grace or is he requesting that God send it? What is the result of this grace, and how does it relate to peace? Such questions of course miss the point of the verse completely, which is simply to greet the church rather than to create theological discussion. But it is one case of the way the word "grace" is used in different contexts. One more example comes from Romans 7:25, translated in the NIV as "Thanks be to God, who delivers me through Jesus Christ our Lord". The word "thanks" is a translation of *charis*, grace, which is here offered by Paul to God as a result of the experience of salvation.

Experience seems to be the key in considering grace in the Bible, linked to the covenants of God with his people. There are two related phrases that I use about grace that seek to reflect this: grace is any act that springs from a covenantal bond of love; and, more briefly, grace is what spirit does. In the first, we see that many different actions when performed in a covenantal sense are acts of grace – mercy, forgiveness, charity, love. Not every act of mercy is an act of grace, since anyone can be merciful, but when it springs from covenantal love then it takes on the nature of grace. A good example of this would be my wife's mercy when yet again I forget to sort out the loft so that she can find things that have been hidden up there for years – one of many graces that I receive all too often.

Grace is present in the Bible from the earliest chapters, as it is revealed in creation itself and then transformed and expanded as soon as sin enters the picture. God, being complete in himself, does not need creation or humankind, but in the act of creation there is a bond or covenant that involves many blessings, many examples of grace, in beauty and provision and relationship and many other things. Even after sin, much of this grace continues to be present: often known as common grace – that which all people experience in any time or place.

With the advent of sin, new types of grace are necessary, beginning with the mercy of a holy God in not destroying anything contaminated by sin and continuing in the presence of God by his Spirit, the promise of salvation, and new covenantal bonds through which grace can be exhibited. None of this is deserved, since the wages of sin is death, and thus any Christian consideration of humanity, let alone salvation and a new life, must begin with grace, and any goodness that is present must be viewed as a result of God's grace.

When we speak of the grace of God, the "active agent" is always the Holy Spirit, the manifest power and presence of God in creation, the Spirit of God the Father, who is revealed in the New Testament also to be the Spirit of Christ. Hence Paul requests grace from the Father and the Son because it is a work of the one Spirit of one God.

One major confusion that the church today seems to suffer from regards the fact that grace tends to be applied more to the Son than to the Spirit. This at once brings up two major points of concern, the first relating to the work of the Son and an understanding of the atonement that was accomplished in the incarnation and at the cross and whose power was demonstrated in the resurrection. This is the core work of the incarnate Word of God, overcoming the power of sin and death and allowing for a restored relationship between humankind and God. However, unless you hold that everyone is saved –

universalism – then this is insufficient in itself for salvation without each person experiencing a work of grace, a work of the Holy Spirit.

Here is the beginning of the second problem, an understanding of the Christian experience of God. Joining grace into the work of atonement and associating it primarily with Christ can create problems for understanding our new lives with God. If grace is linked to Christ, there are two possible results: either grace is historically located at the Christ event, which with its assurance of salvation leaves me twiddling my thumbs until he comes again; or Christ is present with me now, which denies the ascension. Both of these have major knock-on effects regarding our understanding of the Holy Spirit, as we shall see.

A former student of mine, Rich Powney, worked on the ascension and uncovered what seems to be a massive hole in our understanding of God, and all being well a popular book on that topic will be published soon to challenge the church. As a taster for that and to cover what is necessary here, it seems that many in the church disagree with Christ's statement in John's Gospel that it is better for him to go away so that the Spirit can come. This is confirmed by the number of times I hear the phrase "Jesus is with me". The ascension means that Christ is not with us – except by his Spirit, which is something very different – but is continuing his work in the heavenly realms. If the focus remains so closely on Christ and his work, then the Spirit can become an optional extra, an app that one might wish to install but not essential hardware, and it should be apparent that this is not in line with what Scripture teaches.

The Spirit of God, sent by the Father and by the Son, is the continuing, effective presence of God in our lives, realizing the salvation won at the cross, transforming us into the likeness of

Christ, gifting us for the work we are called to, and guaranteeing our life to come. All of these are aspects of the grace of God at work in our lives and none are optional for the Christian. There is no set-up in which we can have saving faith in what Christ has done and then sit and wait for the benefits of this when we die. If we have this faith, then we have the Holy Spirit working in us, with us, and through us, and this necessitates a dynamism in who we are – in growing holiness – and in what we do – in exhibiting the fruits of the Spirit and in sacrificial service of others.

The major Christian writers in the first few centuries grasped this wonderfully. They did not spend much time writing systematic theologies, but rather helped the church to understand the impact of what Christ had done and their ongoing experience in troubled times, guarding faith in this revelation against teachings that would take away the core of the faith. There was thus no textbook or even structured writing on either grace or the Holy Spirit, but both were integral to all aspects of the Christian life. Grace in particular was always present in three areas linked to the work of the Holy Spirit: salvation, sanctification, and gifting.

The focus therefore continued to be on the experiential nature of grace, and this would continue to the end of the fourth century. The lack of systematic thought was linked to the Holy Spirit, who was the key to every aspect of Christian faith and life but whose nature had not been closely examined. This is shown in the first version of the Nicene Creed, written in 325, which contained a concise clause on the Father that remained unchanged, a thorough understanding of the person and work of the Son that would be further developed, and a rather brief third section on the belief of the church that can be quoted in full: "And in the Holy Spirit". Given how closely

Spirit and grace were tied together, the paucity of this section shows how undeveloped Christian thought was in this area.

AUGUSTINE

Augustine of Hippo (354–430) changed all this for the Western Church, earning the title "Doctor of Grace" (what a great title!) for transforming the understanding of grace. In his early writings, Augustine reads very much like his predecessors, but this changes later, and I would highlight two factors behind this change: a consideration of his own experience of conversion; and the dispute that developed with Pelagius.

When reading any Christian work, it is good to know something of the life of the writer, as their experience will naturally inform how they think about the faith. Augustine grew up in a Christian home – at least, we know that his mother had a strong faith – but he rebelled against this upbringing, giving himself up to many pleasures and then devoting himself to a religion called Manicheanism, which focused on purity of spirit above and sometimes against the flesh. Augustine was an opponent of Christianity until he came into contact with Ambrose, Bishop of Milan, and through this experienced a grace that he neither sought nor deserved. He reflects on this in his most famous work, the *Confessions*. This experience of rejecting the faith and then being brought back by the power of grace led him to explore the nature of grace more fully than any writer before him.

This project became more urgent for Augustine when he heard about the teachings of a British monk, Pelagius, who arrived in Rome around AD 400. Pelagius came from a Celtic background that put a great stress on morality and the responsibility of humankind in responding to grace. This led to a focus on external grace in creation, the law, the Bible, and the church over internal grace through the Holy Spirit, possibly even to the exclusion of internal grace. Augustine saw that this exalted humanity far too greatly in comparison with biblical teaching on the sovereignty of God, with the power of internal grace vital to his response.

A presentation of Augustine's writing on grace could easily fill several books, so the focus here will be on aspects that set up the development of thought through the medieval period, leading to the discussions that resulted in the Reformation. Only via this route can we understand the various nuances in the positions held by different reformers and how they sought to return the church's teachings to their perceived roots.

Apparently, one should start at the very beginning, and so we need to deal with original sin and its ongoing effects on humanity. This concept had always been present in the church, but Augustine developed it in important ways, particularly in regard to the status of children. Whereas before Augustine the prevalent thought had been that there was sufficient grace to provide salvation for infants, Augustine required a specific grace through baptism to deal with the effects of original sin – hence a chapter in his work entitled "Unbaptised Infants Damned, But Only Lightly". This construct changed the nature of faith and the role of the church in the life of an individual from this point on.

A second area of Augustine's thought that warrants attention concerns his ideas on phases of grace, a few of which should be presented here. These start with what is called prevenient grace, which means grace that comes before any response. The first movement in salvation is one of grace that awakens the human will to the knowledge of good and gives it the capacity to respond to the call of God. This is consistent with most of the writing both before and since Augustine. The next grace that needs noting is efficient grace, which is effective in accomplishing the desired result in directing the human will, resulting in a saving faith; without this grace, it is not possible to be saved. From this point, a person experiences cooperating grace, where grace works with the will, guiding and transforming it through the trials of life. Connected to this, and of vital importance, is persevering grace, which continues to the end of life. There is a lot of talk in the church today about assurance of salvation, but Augustine warns against such a notion regarding the future. One can be confident of faith today, but only the receipt of persevering grace to the end will result in the life to come.

Thirdly, we need to be aware of Augustine's thought on venial and mortal sins, together with his ideas about purgatory, in order to understand developments on grace in the following centuries. Purgatory seems a difficult concept for most Protestants today to envisage, let alone understand, but the roots are in understanding biblical teaching about death and judgment. Judging from discussions with students, most people seem to take their belief about what happens when we die from Jesus' words to the thief on the cross, "Today you will be with me in paradise", indicating an immediate transfer from old creation to new creation. Yet there are many passages to indicate that the final "destination" is decided on a judgment day at the end of time, when all will be raised and there will be a separation of sheep and goats. Seeking to honour these passages, the early church held to various forms of intermediate state between this life and the life to come, and Augustine's teaching on purgatory as a place of purification was one strand of this line of thought. Connected to this were his developments of ideas on different types of sin, venial and mortal: the first requiring confession and forgiveness without losing salvation; the second with eternal consequences.

It is important to remember that Augustine is trying through these teachings both to honour passages in the Bible that indicate an intermediate state and a forgiveness/purification after this life (such as Matthew 12:32 and 1 Corinthians 3:10–15) and to encourage a spirituality that emphasizes holiness and humility in the receipt and exercise of grace. Evangelicals do not follow Augustine in his definitions of types of sin or the existence of purgatory, but the fact that a thinker and writer as great as Augustine taught them shows the complexity of this area of thought and might encourage humility as we discuss ideas with those who disagree with us.

THE MEDIEVAL PERIOD

Augustine was writing at a time of transition in the Roman empire, after Christianity had been accepted and while it was growing but before saturation point when almost all would be baptized, a situation that was realized in the centuries after he died. His understanding of grace spoke to unbelievers of the power of God and the need to submit to his grace, while church members were given a security in the power of baptismal grace and an urgency to live in cooperative grace in order to receive salvation when they died.

Soon after Augustine's death, the nature of Western society and the place of the church within it changed dramatically, leading to a transformed experience of Christianity. With the fall of the Western Roman empire and the shattering of political unity, life changed. The *pax Romana* (Roman peace) had underpinned the development of civilization – economy, towns, education (for a complete list, see Monty Python's "What have the Romans ever done for us?") – and the end of this led to a loss of wealth and stability. The vast majority of the population were left farming the land to produce enough to survive, while war and invasion were ever-present dangers. The only unifying factor left was the church, which provided a solid foundation for this life and a guarantee of life to come. With expectations of and experience in this life severely diminished, eternal identity grew greatly in importance.

What did this mean for the understanding of grace? Firstly, the new, small political entities sought a stronger unity of identity, and religion played a key role in this. The faith of the king was determining for the faith of the people, who were not equipped or encouraged to question details of their beliefs. This became an important factor in the spread of Christianity during this period in the Anglo-Saxon kingdoms of England and then in missions to Germany and Scandinavia. For those who took on Christianity, infant baptism became a near-universal practice, along with Augustine's understanding of the effects of this on the penalty of original sin.

The grace that leads to salvation, prevenient grace, and that which effects salvation, efficient grace, thus worked in a person before they were even able to speak. Only if they committed a sin so grave that they would lose salvation, as Augustine believed was possible with mortal sins, was there a need to bring these people back to the state of grace. The teaching of the church therefore focused from childhood onwards on the need to engage with cooperating and persevering grace to guard a person through the trials of life and to prepare them for the life to come. Eucharist or Communion was vital in the communication of this grace, while there was a great increase in the emphasis on confession and penance since, if all receive grace and the Spirit at baptism, the role of the church is to emphasize the realization of the effects of this in growing holiness through life. In line with Augustine's denial of assurance unless one perseveres in grace, the sign of such perseverance was in taking Communion, in following the teaching of Christ through the church, and in practices that encouraged the pursuit of holiness.

Having mentioned baptism, Communion, and penance, this seems a good place to outline the teaching on the sacraments that was essential to the medieval understanding of grace. There were ultimately seven recognized sacraments: baptism, confirmation, Eucharist, reconciliation (confession), anointing the sick, Holy Orders, and marriage. Each of these was held to be a biblically affirmed instrument of specific aspects of God's grace, with a different grace experience in the various sacraments. Instruments of grace did not have any innate spiritual power in themselves, but were appointed by God as practices for the church through which the Holy Spirit would act in the lives of believers. The active agent in the sacraments was always the Holy Spirit, though at times this may not have been immediately clear to recipients, owing partly to a lack of sufficient teaching and partly to the theatrical presentation that seemed to communicate that the power was in the church or the priest. The purpose of the sacraments was to tie believers into the church and an experience of grace through all the stages of life; the result at times seems to have been an overt religiosity that cloaked the need for faith.

At no point did the medieval church teach that salvation could be achieved through human endeavour alone. The confrontation between Augustine and Pelagius fixed their understanding on the need for grace and faith. Here is one example from Thomas Aquinas that shows the extent of the perceived need for grace:

Humans on their own can in no way rise from sin without the help of grace. For since sin is working in an action and remains in the guilt that results, to rise from sin is not the same as to cease the act of sin. To rise from sin means that a person has restored what they lost by sinning. This is a triple loss, the stain of sin, the corruption of their natural goodness and the debt of punishment. The stain blemishes the brightness of grace through the deformity of sin. Natural goodness is corrupted inasmuch as a person's nature is disordered by their will not being subject to God. When this order is overthrown, the consequence is that the whole nature of sinful humanity remains disordered. Lastly, there is the debt of punishment, inasmuch as sinful humanity deserves everlasting damnation. Now it is clear that none of these three can be restored except by God. For since the brightness of grace results from the shedding of divine light, this cannot be brought back unless God sheds his light anew. Therefore a new and residing gift is necessary, and this is the light of grace. Likewise, nature can only be restored, i.e. the will can only be subject to God, when God draws the will to himself by grace. Finally, the guilt of eternal punishment can only be remitted by God, against whom the offence was committed and who is the judge of all. Therefore, in order that people might rise from sin, there needs to be the help of grace, both as an ongoing gift and through the internal work of God.

(Translated and edited by the author from the
Summa Theologica, book 2, question 109, article 7.)

Augustine was the key thinker in Western theology, and, as the "Doctor of Grace", his influence remained firm. The problem became the role of this teaching as it dripped down from the church's doctrine to the believer's experience. One may be able to understand why, in a society so dominated by Christianity and influenced by the church, the focus in ministry shifted from how to be saved (which was accomplished through baptismal grace) to how to live as a Christian as a member of the church and in the ongoing work of the Holy Spirit. Practically, what many inferred was a sense that the deposit of the Holy Spirit that had been received needed building on through human investment in order to realize salvation.

The emphasis on purgatory as it developed from Augustine was important in this. If eternal salvation was won through baptismal grace and could not be lost except through extreme (mortal) sin, then the after-death effects of cooperating grace must relate to the experience of the intermediate state. This could create a fear in the minds of believers about what was to come and/or an intention to work sufficiently hard to avoid potential penalties and punishments.

A key word in this process is "merit", which is particularly prominent in the writing of Thomas Aquinas and has been important in much Catholic thought ever since. The word in relation to humankind and grace implies an earning, by people, of grace, although this is not necessarily a correct understanding, since any right human thought, word, or deed that would carry merit is a result of a movement of God's grace in a person, which Aquinas calls the "principle" of all merit. From this come a wide spread of writings, ranging from those that emphasize the grace that leads to "meritorious" action to those that do not explicitly acknowledge this role of grace and imply a purely human endeavour.

The teaching on indulgences was one area where there was a resulting confusion, concerning grace at least, and at times what appeared to be a replacement of grace. The roots of this o back to the early centuries and an idea that the church as the body of Christ inhabited by the Spirit of Christ was in some mystical way the instrument of grace through which Christ's victory over sin was realized in a person's life. Through the medieval period the mystical element of this diminished as theology sought greater understanding, and in this process grace seems to have taken on a more substantial sense rather than being primarily the transforming and empowering experience of earlier Christianity. Indulgences were at times the greatest realization of this, with grace seemingly bought and sold. This was not related primarily to eternal salvation but to purgatory and the path to ultimate salvation after death, although such a distinction was unlikely to have been made in people's minds. There was an almost mathematical side to grace by the high medieval period, when one could calculate the length of time endured in purgatory for any given set of sins, and therefore the cost of the grace of indulgences necessary to cover this.

Augustine's ideas on grace were never lost to the church, and throughout the medieval period there were writers particularly in the realm of spirituality who retained a rich understanding of the work of God in every aspect of a person's life. The teaching on saving grace being experienced through baptism led to a strong emphasis on the life that was lived after this and the sins that were committed, however, and this was easily understood as righteousness and salvation that were earned rather than received. There was a desperate need for reform in this area, but what should such reform focus on?

REFORMATION THOUGHT

Here we will focus on the three most distinctive and lasting contributions on grace in the early sixteenth century, starting with that of Luther, who sat solidly in the historic Catholic tradition, then looking at Calvin's work, and finishing with the Catholic reforming Council of Trent. One area that was generally taught by protesting groups highlighted the importance of grace granting "imputed" righteousness over "imparted" righteousness. The two terms refer to the righteousness of Christians, with the former indicating that the only important righteousness is Christ's, which clothes Christians and makes them acceptable to God; the latter focuses on the righteousness that is created in a person by the work of the Holy Spirit.

It is worth noting that there is one relevant document agreed by representatives of both sides (Lutherans for the Protestants), at Regensburg in 1541, that uses both terms, initially concentrating on imputed righteousness but affirming imparted (more precisely, inherent) righteousness as a work of the Holy Spirit in the Christian. With this exception, documents increasingly taught one or other result of grace; the Council of Trent condemned a view that held only to Christ's righteousness and indicated no role for grace making a person in any way righteous, a view that few reformers would have shared, since their doctrine of salvation always upheld Augustine's cooperative or persevering grace as an essential part of the Christian life. Unfortunately, in popular thought today there often seems to be a dichotomy created between the two views, as if belief in one negates the possibility for any concept of the other, yet inheritors of the Reformation such as Thomas Hooker and Jonathan Edwards taught a twofold righteousness.

Luther

As far as grace is concerned, Luther is perhaps most famous for confronting the practice of indulgences in the form that it had reached by the early sixteenth century. The breaking point for Luther was the building of St Peter's Church in Rome and the role of the sale of indulgences in relation to this, which formed the focus of his famous 95 Theses that are seen as kicking off the Reformation.

In many ways, however, this precise instance was more a surface issue that exemplified a developing understanding of grace in which Luther's own experience was more transformative. This deeper thought was closely linked to the doctrine of justification by faith alone, which we will look at in the next chapter. The reason why the teaching on faith that Luther found in the book of Romans had such a great impact was his reception of the medieval concept of merit in relation to grace.

Luther was taught a theology that was heavily influenced by Aristotle, as Aquinas had been (this was not the only stream of thought present in Catholicism at that time), and he imbibed the idea that one was required to engage in works in order to be worthy of salvation, where Augustine had taught that one received eternal life as a result of a grace-inspired life.

Augustine's earlier phases of grace seemed to Luther to have faded far into the background. In order to earn this grace, Luther engaged in self-flagellation, among other spiritual disciplines, to the extent that the Superior of his monastery advised him to devote himself to teaching theology because his spiritual exercises were deemed harmful.

Luther taught both the Bible and Augustine at university and revived in his setting a teaching that grace was sufficient for salvation, with human endeavour necessary as a result of grace. Following this, the believer had a struggle to engage with the continuing sinful self, but for this life would then be "both just and a sinner" (*simul justus et peccator* is Luther's famous phrase), the former a state before God and the latter an ever-present Christian experience.

I am not sure why Luther is not more closely associated with grace. Part of the reason may be that his faith teaching tends to overshadow all other areas. Another reason may be that, in some areas, Luther was very Catholic in his understanding of the work of grace. This was particularly the case regarding the sacraments and the role of the church. Luther only fully affirmed two of the sacraments, baptism and Eucharist, but held that these were designated instruments of grace through the church. His view of the role of the church in grace extended to confession, where, although he promoted a greater emphasis on the believer's direct engagement with God, he did advocate confessing sins in church rather than in private.

Luther's teaching on grace can be better understood from two conflicts that resulted, firstly with Desiderius Erasmus and secondly with Andreas von Karlstadt. Erasmus and Luther had been sympathetic towards each other in an agreed awareness that the church needed reform, but Erasmus continued to believe that such reform was possible under the leadership of the pope, whereas Luther increasingly despaired of this.

In relation to grace, the two disagreed on the nature and role of the human will, with Erasmus arguing strongly that it was a human decision whether or not a person responded to grace in salvation, seeking a middle position between the absolute role of grace inherited from Augustine and the dangers of a purely human work that stemmed from Pelagius. Luther wrote an extensive reply to Erasmus's views in a work entitled *On the Bondage of the Will*, in which he asserted that, while people have a choice regarding what is under them (what they do with their lives), with regard to what is above them (God) the will is bound unless it is released by grace. Luther believed that Erasmus's teachings affirmed that humankind in itself could merit rewards from God, and he therefore rejected any kind of "middle position", but insisted on a line drawn from Augustine that salvation is possible only as the result of a powerful work of grace in a person's life. This shows that Luther sought a greater humility in relation to salvation than he found in much current thought at the time, calling himself a "theologian of the cross", opposing the "theology of glory" that he saw in the work of others.

A second important dispute over grace was with Luther's former friend Andreas von Karlstadt. Karlstadt advocated a more dynamic view of grace than Luther, dissatisfied with the immutability of the sacraments and the incomplete work of salvation that left a Christian, in Luther's view, both justified and yet a sinner. Against this, Karlstadt taught that the Christian was "both good and bad" (*simul bonus et malus*) and that the ongoing work of the Holy Spirit was to eradicate the bad to make a person perfectly good.

Karlstadt's theology freed the Christian from close ties to the church and even from a legalism that he perceived regarding

Scripture. In comparing himself with Luther, Karlstadt claimed that those in Wittenberg (he himself had been thrown out of the city by this stage) were "theologians of the word", a worthy but limited endeavour, whereas he and his followers were "theologians of the Spirit". Luther wanted to stress the power of grace, but Karlstadt went far too far here and Luther responded by calling his opponents back to the revelation of God in the Bible as the validating witness to the experience of grace through the Spirit.

We see here how Luther was very much the reformer, seeking to bring the church back to the core of its teaching when historical, cultural, and church developments had changed at least how grace was perceived by Christians in his time. Luther was not seeking something new and was wary of those who would challenge the church in an attempt to either elevate humanity, as Erasmus did, or to throw out spiritual babies with the suspicious bathwater, which Karlstadt was seen to do.

Calvin

There was certainly a case for including Zwingli in this section, but much of his work follows Luther in calling the church back to Augustine (with the exception of his writing against the sacraments), while his book *On the Providence of God* does not explicitly speak about grace as much or as clearly as Calvin does in the *Institutes of the Christian Religion* and elsewhere.

John Calvin does need to be here because he takes up Luther's thought and extends it in a more systematic fashion. Thus Calvin's thought is often foundational for Protestant views on grace, although there seems to be great freedom to pick and choose which elements can be dropped and where concentration can be shifted. Calvin's extensive positive work on the sacraments, for instance, is often overlooked, despite the core role of these in the believer's experience of God in Calvin's thought. Two elements of Calvin's work on grace will be briefly presented here, although as with all areas in this chapter this is only a sample of the whole.

Firstly, Calvin has a similar opponent to Luther's Erasmus in Pighius, who likewise taught a high view of free choice in salvation rather than focusing on grace. Calvin's response is substantial and, as with Luther, shows him to be for reform rather than a new beginning as he works with the history of Christian thought on grace from the early church through to the medieval period, highlighting strengths and weaknesses, with Augustine generally at the core of the good stuff, but critically engaging with an incredible breadth of different thinkers. As a result there is little new in the book called *The Bondage and Liberation of the Will*, but it is worth noting that Calvin's theology requires that the humble believer live out the results alongside the continuing grace of God.

One aspect of grace that Calvin emphasizes more strongly than any writer since Augustine (although it is a vital element in much medieval theology) is the sovereignty of God. Often this is associated with the doctrine of predestination – in many Christian minds, Calvin and predestination seem to be tied together – but Calvin himself focuses far more attention on the providence of God before later looking at predestination as one of the developments of this core idea. There is an important if subtle distinction here, since providence as Calvin sees it pictures God as present in all times and active by his grace, a more Genesis 2 God engaged with his creation, absolutely balanced with the God of Genesis 1, apart from the creation and creating order out of chaos; later work on predestination seems to emphasize the latter at the expense of the former.

Both are important for Calvin and in both the sovereignty of God and the power of grace over a helpless human will are dominant themes. However, while the later work on predestination could carry the danger of presenting a God planning out history in advance and then merely following it through, the earlier material on providence demonstrates that God's sovereign will is worked out in and through his relationship with a world complicated by sin and rebellion.

The Council of Trent

The Catholic considerations at the Council of Trent covered the area of justification in Session Six, in 1547. One senses when reading the clauses that, while there is much constructive thought present, some sections are framed largely in reaction to what Catholics thought Protestants were teaching.

The Council of Trent clearly teaches the necessity of grace for salvation: "If anyone says that a person may be justified before God by their own works, whether through human nature or through the law, without the grace of God through Jesus Christ, let them be condemned." The grace of God prepares a person for salvation and gives that person the ability to respond to grace. However, the writers at Trent were concerned that humanity might be assigned a purely passive part in salvation in some protesting thought, which seemed to imply that salvation is forced on people regardless of their will and is impossible for others who may wish to be saved. This seemed to go too far in the light of Bible passages that speak of an offer of salvation that requires a response: "I stand at the door and knock; whoever opens the door, I will come and live with them."

As a result, while stating that grace is essential, the Council of Trent also affirms a person's response: "If anyone says that human free will moved and excited by God ... in no way co-operates towards preparing itself for obtaining the grace of Justification, that it cannot refuse its consent if it would but that, as something inanimate, it does nothing whatever and is merely passive, let him be condemned."

In the teachings of Calvin and Trent we see views that seek to protect believers from perceived dangers, and both are working with biblical texts to support them. Calvin is concerned that, once a person is given any active role in the receipt of grace, a works-based or merited model of salvation could develop that would question the sovereignty of God; the Council of Trent addresses a model of salvation that, in removing any active human agency, could seem to eliminate human responsibility and lead to a lazy, inactive Christian life. In reality, both sides seem driven by biblical concepts and thus worthy motives, while both would tend to fall at times into the dangers that can be identified.

Importantly for the sixteenth-century Protestant Church looking at the Proceedings of the Council of Trent, language of merit continued to be included as this Council favoured Thomas Aquinas's presentation of grace over the language of an Augustine or Peter Lombard. This was red-flag language at the time and continued to be a major separating factor for several centuries. Interestingly, in 1999 a Joint Declaration on Justification was published by the Catholic Church and the Lutheran World Fellowship that sought to communicate the essential unity of the two approaches while recognizing a continued use of language by each side that made the other uncomfortable. The statement issued after these meetings sought to clarify the different emphases that underpinned the different language and, while not all in either camp (or those with other views looking at the results of the discussion) were satisfied with the final statement, it was good to see Christians working to understand each other rather than dividing and judging because of an apparent, possibly real, difference in how the beliefs of the church are expressed.

CONCLUSION

This has been a wide sweep through some of what I see as key elements in the history of Christian thought up to and including the Reformation on the complex topic of grace. It has been at a surface level owing to space, but I hope this brief introduction shows some of the depths that are available when exploring grace.

My favourite period for this is the early church, when the dynamic experience was paramount and there had not yet been time to create systematic thought. Augustine's situation both personally and in responding to the teaching of others led him into some wonderful reflections on the nature and role of grace. Sadly, one result of this seems to be that grace took on a more substantial nature and some of the dynamism was lost.

To a certain extent, the Protestant reformers sought to recover that life of grace. Take this passage from Calvin's *Institutes*: "It seems that the grace of God is the rule of the Holy Spirit, in directing and governing the human will. He can only govern by correcting, reforming, renovating (so we say that the beginning of regeneration consists in us losing all we have); in the same way, he cannot govern without moving, impelling, urging, and restraining." It seems, however, that as

Protestant thought developed and was systematized, much of the life was again lost.

We have seen a new revival of active grace in the charismatic renewal. There are lessons from history in the dangers that Luther identified in Karlstadt's free grace, but most of all as the movement develops, when considering the workings of Spirit and grace, there is the danger of creating boxes that unintentionally restrict the power of the grace of our God.

CHAPTER FOUR

THE HUMAN RESPONSE:
FAITH, BELIEF, WORKS

We have seen how deep and broad the church's understanding of grace has been in its development – from the dynamic, experiential grace of the early church, through Augustine's systematic work with a strong sacramental element that became more substantial through the medieval period, and then on to the reformers' emphasis on the sovereignty of God. We now turn to an exploration of elements of the human response to salvation and how the various concepts of faith, works, and belief have been taught by the church in the light of the understanding of grace, so that we can understand different positions better, appreciate some of the complexities involved in relating these ideas, and become aware of weaknesses in spirituality that can result. Unfortunately, in response to some perceived error on the part of another group, fixed ideas and phrases have been generally adopted by some in the church and used as rules to judge, and even condemn, other Christians, placing theological positions above the one body of Christ. I fear that that body spends too much time beating itself up over "certainties" in matters where we cannot have complete comprehension. It is important to gain a clearer understanding of what our brothers and sisters believe and why they have reached that position, and this should help us to be gracious where we see weaknesses, and also to reflect that we too will have areas where others could discern flaws. This may encourage humility before one another and before God, and a first focus on loving God and neighbour rather than on seeking to prove theological superiority or condemning perceived faults.

Faith and belief can seem synonymous in Christian talk, and such a view may cause great problems when considering the major Reformation theme of salvation by faith alone. Faith will be treated here as the core orientation of a person; that which motivates their worship and affects how they live life. It does not necessarily include a great deal of understanding, especially for the earliest church, for churches living in societies that lack any education system, and for the young.

This is where belief comes in, as the processed understanding of the Christian revelation that helps people to grasp the nature of God, creation, humankind, and salvation with the intention of supporting, extending, and enriching faith. Faith and belief are related and should be complementary, but belief demands the engagement of the human mind whereas faith may at times simply rely on wisdom being in the mind of God. In some languages the difference can be less clear because the same word is translated as either faith or belief, so prepositions are often used to differentiate between a more purely rational element (belief, in my method) and what the reformers called a living faith that is informed but more dynamic, and comes from the heart/soul of a person.

Works are the practical living out of the faith in love of God and neighbour, and should be a response to the grace that has been received rather than an attempt to secure grace. Whereas faith is a gift of God and simply the result of grace, belief and works involve the cooperation of the person with the ongoing grace of God as they seek to know God better and to live in his service. Thus there is a danger in both that the role of the person becomes dominant and the help of God is minimized, while the faith that inspires the quest for belief and acts of service can get lost in the background if these are not directed clearly towards the worship of God.

We will also consider the role of human free will during the time of the Reformation, since the nature and extent of the human will affects how a person engages with the grace that they have received in their faith, the development of their beliefs, and their lives working out their salvation.

As before, we will look at the history of the church to discover some of the roots of the practices and understandings of these concepts that become the focus of Reformation discussions. Unlike grace, which is a specific theme throughout the history of Christian thought, the concepts of faith, belief, and works are present in the thought and life of the church without necessarily being explicitly defined or discussed. It is possible, however, to discern the changing thought and practices of the church through the centuries that led to the debates of Reformation times.

EARLY CHURCH

Faith was clearly at the forefront of the identity and nature of the early church. Not that the church was without beliefs – we see in the New Testament the vital place of belief that Christ was the Son of God who died and rose again, that Christ was the messiah promised in the Hebrew scriptures, and that the resurrected Christ would return to bring all things to an end and initiate resurrection life for all who believed in him.

There was not a massive amount of understanding behind these wonderful beliefs, however, but rather a faith that Christ was somehow the "Son" of God and that his death and resurrection were effective for the salvation of all. It soon becomes clear when looking at the church in its first few centuries that there were questions that needed addressing if Christians were to retain a true faith in God and his plan of salvation, since it was not difficult for this to be corrupted by well-intentioned people who allowed their cultural understanding to affect the faith they received.

Two areas stand out as core aspects of the faith that were nearly lost to the church. The first is the nature of humanity, with Greek-thinking Christians following their society's ideas that the spirit is fully pure and the body ultimately mortal and unimportant. This thinking affected the church greatly – sadly, it is alive and well again in churches with ideas of a future spirit existence – and the main battle raged until the work of Irenaeus of Lyon towards the end of the second century. He showed the church that such a view denies creation, incarnation, and resurrection (three pretty important areas of the Christian faith!) and challenged the church to align its view of humanity with that of the Bible, rather than with the ideas of the surrounding society.

A second area was the nature of the Christ, which took a lot longer to sort out, the main definition not coming until AD 451 at the Council of Chalcedon. For 400 years, ideas in the church bounced back and forth between a primarily human Christ with a divine spirit and a divine Christ in a human shell or appearance. The idea of true incarnation, that Christ was somehow both fully human and fully divine, conceived by the Holy Spirit of the Virgin Mary, and that the God-man died on the cross, challenged people's ideas of God too strongly. But this was the faith that needed protection, even if its expression in beliefs was yet to be worked out.

For a couple of centuries, the composition of the church encouraged this simple focus on faith because congregations primarily comprised those who were less well educated – we noted earlier that Christians were condemned as unthinking, simple people by the philosopher Celsus in the late second century. Two of the great strengths of the church from its earliest years were the communities created and the services rendered as people sought to put their faith into practice. At the core of this was a great desire for holiness that is seen in early Christian writings as the defining characteristic of churches, for which members should always strive.

This is linked to the understanding of grace that had been present from the earliest times, as the threefold work of salvation, sanctification, and empowerment, with none of the three being present on its own. There is a strong sense in early church writings that believers are responsible for living out the salvation that God has secured for them. The situation of the church in a sometimes antagonistic, pagan Roman society reinforced this, with times of persecution when the choice to continue in faithful living carried a massive cost. When threatened with death, the victory that Christ has won does not appear before one's eyes, but rather one must have faith that the reality of that victory will soon be experienced in eternal life.

From the third century, things begin to change as the church grows and the amount and quality of thought about the Christian faith increases dramatically. Together with the conversion of the emperor Constantine, this leads to the development of the major creeds of the Christian church – statements of what we believe – and also to greater understanding of the Christian faith more widely. In the East, where most of the work was done, the more mystical/philosophical approach of thinkers led to a continued strong emphasis on faith associated with the core beliefs, and then a space under this where thinking Christians could discuss non-essential matters safely. This has continued to be the approach of Eastern Orthodox Christianity down to today.

The West receives the creeds of the church and develops some Christian thought – with Augustine, of course, at the centre of this – but the break-up of the Roman empire and the changing nature of society in the ensuing centuries affect the progress of the church in this area and, as with the subjects of previous chapters, alter the church's teaching and practice regarding our current themes of faith, belief, and works.

THE MEDIEVAL PERIOD

We have already seen the extent and power of Augustine's thought on grace. For our current themes, we need to recognize that salvation is entirely the work of God and that this is communicated to the individual by the Holy Spirit, with a powerful role for baptismal grace and an essential need for persevering grace to work with the person to complete God's work. Augustine wrote a lot of work on a range of theological topics, but we must leave that for a short time while we look at the church in the 600 years following his death.

This is the period commonly known as the Dark Ages, when there was certainly not much great thought present in the

Western Church. The belief element was thus less important to most people as illiteracy rates were high and the largely agrarian society had little time or energy for thinking through the deep mysteries of the faith.

Salvation as a work of grace that requires only faith to be effective, and that faith being a gift of God (as Augustine taught) rather than an achievement of the individual, meant that the church's activities focused on promoting and protecting the faith of its believers. Augustine had also taught that baptism as an infant was the sacrament whereby salvation grace was received and the effects of original sin removed, and Western Europe was moving towards Christendom, when the vast majority of the population considered themselves Christian. The result for the church, based on its understanding of Augustine, was that salvation by grace through faith was present in believers from their baptism unless they rejected this later in life. The task of the church was thus to help them to continue in their faith, and the major signs of this were the sacrament of Eucharist, which tied them into the body of Christ, the sacrament of reconciliation, which encouraged people to remain in a state of grace and to recognize the effect of sins committed after baptism on their relationship with God, and the practice of good works, which showed that people were living in persevering grace.

The length of time that this situation lasted – around 600 years – engrained in the church and people of Western Europe a certain approach to faith and works. Because the experience of grace was for most people largely confined to the sacraments, primarily baptism, Eucharist, and reconciliation, the faith that resulted was tied into their concept of church and could become a faith in the church of God as much as in God himself. The works that originally resulted from salvation, in the theology of Augustine, became the major focus of spirituality for many because their salvation had been secured at baptism, as long as they didn't commit a mortal sin that cut them off from the body of Christ.

In the later medieval period when society began to change, from the late eleventh century onwards, the idea of faith in God coming through the church and the essential role of works in the Christian life changed little for the vast majority of Christians, with Scripture, grace, and faith in God to some extent becoming background concepts. Theoretically, these were still essential foundations for the church and its members – and in many medieval lives and writings we can see that they were retained as such – but for some leaders and many lay people they seem to have rather been sidelined and lost their significance.

One area that did develop during this period was that of belief, beginning with Anselm of Canterbury's method of "faith seeking understanding". Here we see a right relationship between faith and belief, with the former as the basis and the latter dependent on this. The early twelfth century saw the formation of the first European universities, which in the north of Europe majored on the study of theology and philosophy. As we saw when considering the church, Scripture and the writings of the Church Fathers were viewed as unquestionable authorities. However, as study progressed through the medieval period and more tools in the form of new ways of thinking about concepts were discovered and developed, the precise questions that were being considered became removed from the concepts and context of the New Testament and the early church, and work seemed to be required to bridge the gap. There is a challenge for the church today in this, with many discussions about how the church relates to current society becoming distant from the earliest church, with the temptation to bridge the gap using modern notions that can corrupt the faith.

During the medieval period, the beliefs of the church expressed at times both by the Vatican and in the universities became separated from the faith of the church and from the majority of Christians as they lived their lives. Unfortunately, most of this developing belief occurred apart from the problems the church was facing as society developed educationally and socially; a progress that highlighted issues resulting from the understanding of church and believer in the centuries after Augustine.

Faith in the church and the working out of this in cooperation with grace were good encouragements during the Dark Ages for people to retain an essential commitment to God in their lives when there was little space or capability for more than this. As society developed, however, people sought a greater understanding of their faith and expected their leaders to stay true to Christian teachings, even to the extent of testing their authenticity. But as the practice of the sacraments developed into sacramental theologies, the dynamics of faith and life became rather lost in calculations of the effects of sin and the quantity of grace that was needed to overcome them.

In lieu of the priority of grace and the simplicity of faith, the language of merit began to gain a major place in talk about the Christian life and destiny. With the doctrine of purgatory gaining in importance throughout the medieval period, the riches that people were encouraged to store up in heaven began to be converted to riches that would limit the time spent in purgatory. While technically the salvation model did not change from salvation by grace through faith, the ultimate ends of this process in infant baptism and resurrection life were obscured by life as a Christian and the anticipation of time in purgatory that came to dominate the popular conception and practice of Christianity.

Faith and Grace

We will not follow a writer-by-writer approach this time but look at the concepts and how they relate to each other. It seems wise to begin with faith, since both "faith alone" and "grace alone" were important ideas for the reformers in regard to salvation, and having two that are "alone" seems a little confusing to say the least. One solution to this that can come across in Christian speech and worship is simply to make the two synonymous or interchangeable. This does justice to neither grace nor faith, however, whereas seeking to understand why each is necessary "alone" in its different way should begin to provide the basis for a humble yet active Christian life.

The concept of grace alone refers to the fact that God is the author and agent of salvation. The universality of sin in humankind means that there is no hope for us unless God chooses to act in providing the means necessary for salvation for all and then reaching out to each individual through multiple paths of grace by his Spirit in order to awaken people to the possibility of forgiveness and to strengthen them to take hold of the salvation on offer. Grace in salvation is the divine action through which, alone, it is possible for a person to be saved.

This should not be confused with faith, which is the human means of receiving the grace that is offered and which alone is necessary to receive salvation, although as we will see a faith that is alone in the Christian gives no assuredness of acceptance by God. Faith is the result of a movement of grace; it does not arise in a person without the prompting of the Holy Spirit but is the key response to the work of grace, as Paul writes in Ephesians 2:8: "For it is by grace you have been saved, through faith – and this is not from yourselves, it is the gift of God."

Grace alone, therefore, is what makes salvation possible and effective; faith is alone in that this is all a person needs to receive grace. There is what has always seemed to me a rather strange debate stemming from the writings of the Reformation about whether humans are active or passive in their faith. The issue arises with the Protestant stress on the sovereign grace of God against a perception that the Catholics were teaching that human action contributed to their salvation. There was a fear that if a person were active even just in receiving grace through faith, this implied that the grace was insufficient in itself.

This motivation is certainly honourable in what it says about the primacy of grace; it is not a new concept, as similar ideas can be found in Augustine, Aquinas, and most other medieval Catholic theologians. However, there is a struggle if this is taken too far in recognizing the many biblical texts that speak of an active faith that is the result of the work of grace. If faith is presented too passively, the relational aspect of the Christian life becomes very hard to grasp and a covenantal God seems to give way to a controlling God. There seems, therefore, to be a need for care not to make faith meritorious in any way, as if we might contribute to our salvation, or to claim that faith is active in the sense that it arises from us rather than being aroused and sustained by grace; but also to assert that there is a responsibility to cooperate with this grace in holding on to and developing our faith through all that God has given us.

FAITH

There is more to consider (there is always more to consider!) that relates to this active/passive faith discussion because faith is about trusting in another and a willingness to humble ourselves in accepting help. Thus any idea of "active faith" is not active in substantial or self-promoting terms but in falling on our knees in worship and a self-confessed lack of ability or sufficiency to meet our own needs.

We are building here towards a comparison of faith and belief, but before that it is good to look at just one model of faith that Jesus provides. In Mark 10:15, Jesus says: "Truly I tell you, anyone who will not receive the kingdom of God like a little child will never enter it." While the word "faith" may not be here, the idea is present since the receipt of the kingdom must refer to grace in some form and this is received through faith. The child image for the believer runs through many New Testament texts with a strong Old Testament background and speaks of trust, delight, and simplicity in regard to the faith attitude of the believer before God.

One of the first roles I try to accept in a new church community, at least for a time, is on the crèche rota. Partly this is because I love babies, but also it is because there I learn about what my faith needs to look like. Spending my weeks studying and teaching theology and philosophy can easily make me forget that my basic position must be as a child of faith trusting in my Father God (and occasionally crying when things don't go my way).

For Luther, this idea was at the centre of the reform that he felt was necessary for the church, which seemed to have lost the core of salvation in the work of grace that needed only an inspired faith as its effect and had replaced this with teaching on the need to merit grace through beliefs and actions. Luther's own experience had been that such a position removed any assurance of salvation from the believer, who would always seek to be deemed worthy of receiving grace. The emphasis on salvation "by faith alone" was thus to remove any sense of the need for Christians to merit or contribute in any way towards their salvation.

Such a view had always been present in Catholic teaching through the medieval period if, as stated earlier, it had been rather buried under other teachings. That it was still held can be seen in two documents that the Catholic Church was involved in. The first was published after discussions in Regensburg with the Lutheran Confession, and this comprised a series of articles on various themes that representatives of both sides agreed on. In Article Five, "The Justification of Man", paragraph four states the following:

> *So it is a reliable and sound doctrine that the sinner is justified by living and efficacious faith, for through it we are pleasing and acceptable to God on account of Christ. And living faith is what we call the movement of the Holy Spirit, by which those who truly repent of their old life are lifted up to God and truly appropriate the mercy promised in Christ, so that they now truly recognise that they have received the remission of sins and reconciliation on account of the merits of Christ, through the free goodness of God, and cry out to God: "Abba Father".*

When the Council of Trent produced its Decree on Justification in 1547, there continued to be a stress on the idea that grace is received solely on the basis of faith:

> *When the Apostle says that a person is justified by*
> *faith and freely, those words are to be understood*
> *in the sense that the perpetual consent of the*
> *Catholic Church has held and expressed, that we are*
> *therefore said to be justified by faith because faith is*
> *the beginning of human salvation, the foundation*
> *and the root of all justification, without which it*
> *is impossible to please God and to come into the*
> *fellowship of his sons. But we are therefore said to*
> *be justified freely because none of those things that*
> *precede justification, whether faith or works, merit*
> *the grace itself of justification. For, if it is a grace, it*
> *is not by works, otherwise, as the same Apostle says,*
> *grace is no more grace.*

One might wonder in view of these passages why there was no reconciliation between the two sides on this point. While the teaching on justification at Regensburg was not warmly accepted by those to whom the delegates returned on either side, there were other issues – principally papal authority and transubstantiation – which were not agreed on at all, while neither side was very happy with the process of discussion and resolution (particularly the Catholic Church), and together these factors meant that Regensburg was rejected as a path towards unity. The Catholic Council of Trent that began soon afterwards reinforced the differences between Catholics and Lutherans. Interestingly, reconciliation has happened in part in the document we mentioned earlier, "Joint Declaration on Justification by Faith" published by the Lutheran Confession and the Catholic Church in 1999, which sought to clarify how the different approaches and principles of the two sides can be held together in one faith, when they did not allow for a united position in the sixteenth century.

One aspect of the Reformation discussions concerns the position of infants before God. The early Greek church had held that sufficient grace had been extended by the work of Christ on the cross to overcome the sin inherited from Adam and to cover infants before they could deliberately sin. Augustine placed a higher view on the impact of sin, arguing that only after baptismal grace was the original penalty overcome. This was the position of the medieval church, although a genuine intention to give or receive baptism was considered effective if a person or child died before the actual act could be carried out.

Given that salvation is by grace through faith, this raises the question of the faith that saves an infant. It relates to the concept of covenant relationship, which involves not only the individual but the whole people with whom the covenant is made. In this view, individual identity, while important, is less important than communal identity – as is still the case in many cultures in the world today. Europe moved towards individualism many centuries ago through various humanist movements and this can create problems when engaging with the more communal cultures that we find in Scripture.

Infants and children were seen as part of the covenant community, as they had been in the Old Testament, and were thus deemed to be part of the faith community because of their parents' faith. This was not sufficient to cover them throughout life; hence the sacraments first of confirmation and then of reconciliation to move young people into their own relationship with cooperating and persevering grace that was considered necessary for salvation.

The major Protestant reformers all upheld the practice of infant baptism, though for different reasons. Luther was the closest to the Catholic belief and practice and argued strongly that infants had faith, if not a good knowledge of what that faith was in or how it led to salvation. As a teacher of Augustine and inspired by him, Luther accepted the effect of baptism in overcoming the punishment inherited via original sin. Zwingli focused less on the precise grace/faith dynamic of infant baptism, but held to the practice on the basis of Scripture (from the baptism of households and from 1 Corinthians 7 that the children of Christian parents are holy) and as a sign of the covenant and thus related to circumcision. It was a sign for Zwingli rather than an instrument of grace, but it was linked to the faith community. Calvin also taught that infant baptism was the right Christian practice in line with the Bible, but maintained that its effect depended on whether the child was one of the elect, which would become apparent over time and after death. An elect child thus might receive grace at baptism whereas one who was not predestined would not, in accordance with the will of God. The Anglican Church under Cranmer retained a close affinity with Catholic practice, emphasizing the need for a right faith, even if one that is supplied by others until the child develops their own.

There were groups in the early sixteenth century who disagreed with all of the above and began the practice of rebaptizing people as adults: the Anabaptists, whom we have met several times already. They were condemned by all of the major groups – Catholics, Lutherans, and Reformed. Luther and Zwingli both had close contact with the Anabaptists and wrote extensive treatises against their practices, but these formed the basis of the baptistic traditions that emphasized personal faith over a community/covenantal concept on the basis of a lack of explicit reference to the practice of infant baptism in Scripture.

BELIEF

All this begins to address a question that I have wondered about, which is how Christians understand the relationship between faith and belief. In particular, in the anniversary year of the Reformation, with the popularity of the phrases associated with that movement, what did people mean when they talked about being saved "by faith alone"? It appears to me that this can easily become synonymous with "by belief alone", at which point there is a real problem.

Luther writes excellently on this, I believe (yes, believe, not have faith). The first point to make is that belief is something that is ours and which we develop, linked to our knowledge and (I hope) under God's guidance, whereas faith is an admission that we have nothing and must simply receive. The quest for belief, and for a good belief given other people's mistakes, is thus at least in part (and possibly wholly) a human endeavour as we work with the revelation of God and, all being well, in cooperation with grace. "I believe" implies a certainty on the part of the one who professes it, whereas "I have faith" indicates a humility that does not need to know fully.

Luther builds on this point in writing about infant baptism. If, he says, we can only get baptized once we have developed a certain faith – with the appropriate belief system – then we may never be baptized, since such certainty of the things of God is unlikely ever to be achieved. Even if for a short time a person is satisfied, the likelihood is that the next day something will occur that will raise more questions and the absolute firmness of belief will be lost. If this happens, should I be baptized again once I am back in my position of certainty? An additional problem with this approach for Luther is that it makes conversion ultimately a human decision – 'I believe or accept Christ' – rather than a divine action of grace.

Belief is thus not the dynamic that receives grace and lays a person in the safe arms of our heavenly Father; that is faith. If this were not the case, would we say about young children or those with severe mental disabilities that they cannot be saved? It took a little while for me, with my strong Christian upbringing and schooling in the faith, to realize that there was no entrance exam at the pearly gates that needed to be passed in order to be admitted into the new creation. I have been to some churches that seem to be preparing the believer for this, gauging a person's standing before God by the beliefs they profess and confusing this with faith.

The morning after I had spoken on this theme at a seminar at Spring Harvest, Paula Gooder gave the Bible teaching from John's Gospel. As part of this, she spoke of two different phrases that John uses in relation to belief that are unfortunately translated the same in English. The first are commands to "believe that", which are the creedal or doctrinal bits of John: for example, Christ is the messiah, the Father has sent the Son. More often, John writes of "believing into", generally translated as "believing in". The difference is important. Believing in something is a static state, a rational assent to a given notion; believing *into* is dynamic, it is experiential; it speaks of a walk if not a leap of faith.

Luther's point is relevant here, speaking of an element that is not often high on the evangelical church agenda: the mystery of the faith. With such a strong history of rational engagement with the Bible and with the world, the focus seems to be on having reasonable answers to any question. The further I delve into theology, the clearer it is that the ultimate answer to most questions becomes: "I don't know." What is more, the more deeply I study the revelation of God, the more I am encouraged to answer with: "I *cannot* know." If I understand the mind, will, and action of God, my God is too small. I love the way Paul regularly, in the midst of his more theological passages, suddenly breaks out in a doxology, a hymn of praise and wonder: "Oh, the depth of the riches of the wisdom and knowledge of God! How unsearchable his judgments, and his paths beyond tracing out!" (Romans 11:33).

Should we then give up on belief? By no means (I would lose my job as a theologian for a start!). But we do need to recognize the role of belief in the Christian life. We are called to worship the Lord our God with all our mind in addition to the rest of our being, and we do this through an engagement with the revelation he has given us. What a revelation it is, in creation, in Christ, in Spirit, in Scripture, in church, in neighbour, and in self! Any of these is worth a book in itself, but I just want to note one example here from my own experience.

When I was at university, I began to struggle with reading the Bible because it just seemed a bit dry. I realize now that this was because I had begun to treat it more as an exercise in English literature than as the living word of God. So many Bible studies gave a text and a series of questions and the task was to find the right answers in the passage. I could learn about God that way and build up or confirm my belief system, but I found it hard to be open to the inspiration of the Spirit breathing through the revelation – this is where we need to recover one aspect of Calvin's teaching on the Bible, namely that the Spirit continues to breathe in interpretation. Now when I look at Scripture I see a wonderful mess because it is the witness of God's grace relationship with his sinful people. It is a wonderfully existential document – not a textbook with easy-to-learn lessons, but filled with stories and experiences, with failures and the odd success – that calls me to wonder at God's patience and mercy and inexhaustible grace in the face of humanity's stubbornness and pride. Now I expect to be shocked and called to change when I read the Bible, and when I'm not I guess that I need to be more open to the voice of the Spirit. In this aspect, Calvin's thought certainly needs to affect me, and possibly the church, more than it has done. We need to hold our beliefs more lightly than the authority of the Spirit to speak through the Scriptures to challenge and extend our concept of God and his work.

When we look at the complexity of our faith and of the sinful world around us, we see that the task of building belief structures for Christianity that we then work through in this changing world is massive and one that is never going to be finally, absolutely completed. Yet we are given minds and the riches of all this revelation and encouraged to worship with those minds as we glimpse the being and work of our God. Theology is rather a strange word – the study of God. Who are we to study God? We are called to do this, but the purpose of such study must be understood – not to comprehend, but to worship more deeply. In addition, we seek belief in order to guard a right experience of faith based on the revelation we have received; hence the need to work at this together as a church across the world, across denominations, and through history.

This brings us to another aspect of Reformation thought on belief: the need for a right belief in line with Scripture and the church. The concept of sound doctrine is something that all the different groups emphasized as they approached each other, and all (except some of the radical Anabaptists) worked extensively with the historical voices from the church to support their teaching. What is somewhat concerning is the fact that, with good motivation and the same sources, there was no major agreement between the different reforming groups; however, given what we have seen of the ultimately incomprehensible nature of God and his action, perhaps this should not be surprising. What is more worrying for the reader of Reformation texts is the language that the various writers use about each other, which is not limited to theological condemnation but gets pretty personal at times. Even given a change in society's attitude to language, we should not seek to defend people we may admire for their desire to stand up for the faith if their conduct is poor, but should accept that even the strongest in faith have weaknesses and learn to examine ourselves and ensure we love God and neighbour not only in what we say but in how we say it.

Belief and faith are therefore not the same thing, and need to be kept distinct. Our first call as Christians is to have faith in God – Father, Son, and Holy Spirit – and to trust that his grace is sufficient. But we are then called on to engage with the revelation of God in our minds, and this should deepen and enrich our faith as we see glimpses of the majesty and wonder of our God and his work in the world. It should give us greater assurance of the power of the faith we profess and should help us to guard against cultural influences that could subtly undermine our faith. We need to be careful, however, that it does not dominate our Christian lives or relieve our need for faith by providing an all-encompassing belief system, and we should remain humble in knowing that our God and his plans are too exalted for us to comprehend fully.

WORKS

If justification is by faith alone, why talk about human works any longer? Clearly this was an issue at the time of the Reformation because of the late medieval emphasis on works. However, the critique of this did not create a sense of liberty for a Christian under the reformers' leadership. While human works may not be a cause of salvation, most agreed that they were an essential result of salvation and that any salvation must be worked out in a Christian's life of holiness and service.

Luther ran into some trouble in the application of his thought early in the Reformation as his followers applied the idea of freedom from the authority of the church to society and sought liberation from their earthly masters. The result was a series of revolts across the German lands that forced Luther to condemn them and then clarify his teaching. In respect of the doctrine of justification by faith alone, Luther parted ways with Andreas von Karlstadt about what this implied for the Christian life. Karlstadt taught that the saved Christian was *simul bonus et malus* ("at the same time good and bad"), and that with work on the latter a person could work towards moral perfection, which is the goal in this life. Luther held that, after justification, the Christian was *simul justus et peccator* ("at the same time justified and a sinner"), implying that the latter was a continuing state that required the Christian to wrestle with their sins throughout life. As a result, Luther continued to teach that confession to a priest was a good practice for Christians, who should strive to train themselves in righteousness, highlighting the danger of self-validation if a person confessed privately to God.

A warning about what could result from too free an approach to reforming the church was represented by those early Anabaptist groups who were involved in violence against their opponents and then advocated immoral practices such as the legalization of polygamy. In this as in most areas, we can see great diversity within the movement collected together under the terms Radical Reformation or Anabaptism, since some of the groups most prioritizing holiness also came under these banners.

One can see that the Catholic Church feared that concentrated teaching on justification by faith alone would lead to a free morality where, after salvation, there was no responsibility to live a holy life. Such a view is condemned in two forms at the Council of Trent as if it were one of the major impacts of Protestant theology on its spirituality:

> *If anyone says that nothing besides faith is commanded in the Gospel; that other things are indifferent, neither commanded nor prohibited, but free; or, that the Ten Commandments in no way apply to Christians, let them be condemned.*

> *If anyone says that a person who is justified and however perfect is not bound to observe the commandments of God and of the Church, but only to believe – as if indeed the Gospel were a bare and absolute promise of eternal life without the condition of observing the commandments – let them be condemned.*

While we are dealing with the Catholic Church, two more points should be made. The first goes back to the Regensburg Agreement. In that agreed statement on justification by faith with the Lutheran Confession, the role of works is clarified thus:

Now those who say that we are justified by faith alone should at the same time teach the doctrine of repentance, of the fear of God, of the judgement of God and of good works, so that all the chief points of the preaching may remain firm, as Christ said: "preaching repentance and the remission of sins in my name" [Luke 24:47]. This is to prevent this way of speaking [i.e. sola fide] from being understood other than has been previously mentioned.

This shows that there were some in the Catholic Church, notably Cardinal Contarini, the major Catholic representative at Regensburg, who had a view of faith and works that was in accord with that of many Protestant thinkers. Yet, when it came to the writing of the Decree on Justification at the Council of Trent, while there were the acknowledgments of the prime roles of faith and grace quoted above, a meritorious role was given to human works:

We must believe that nothing further is wanting to the justified to prevent their being accounted to have, by those very works which have been done in God, fully satisfied the divine law according to the state of this life, and to have truly merited eternal life, to be obtained also in its time, if so be, however, that they depart in grace.

Too much could be made of this section and one must try to balance this theology with the sections that do elevate the roles of grace and faith, but that a person on any basis could be said to have "truly merited eternal life" is language that raises questions about the supremacy of grace.

Turning to John Calvin, the most notable part of his ministry regarding the holy life is the society that developed under his leadership in Geneva. It must be stated at the outset that there is nothing in Calvin that could be interpreted as requiring any human contribution toward salvation apart from the work of God, but the essential working out of this salvation is perhaps more clearly present in Calvin than in any other reformer.

On a practical, lived level, this can be seen in what has become known as the "Geneva experiment", an attempt to create the perfect Christian state. Admirers of Calvin, both today and in the sixteenth century, praise its strict morality and its encouragement through teaching and church discipline. Indeed, at the time many fled to Geneva from persecution elsewhere and wrote in fulsome praise of the society they encountered there. Opponents of Calvin, both today and then (the latter often the native inhabitants of Geneva who had to deal with greatly swelling numbers, all championing the quest for holiness), view Geneva as a religious police state seeking to enforce morality among the population. What is certain about that society is that it showed Calvin's belief in the necessity of sanctification for the Christian and the duty of the church to direct its members towards that goal.

The devotional and applied side of this can be found in Calvin's work *On the Christian Life*, which begins by stating that "no one is a Christian who does not feel some special love for righteousness". The result is a need for Christians to regulate their lives to enable them to be holy, to deny themselves as a core part of their search for holiness, and to focus on the future life and prepare for that time when they will sin no more. While this little book is not about how a person is saved, it is essential for every Christian in Calvin's view – there is no salvation by grace through faith that does not result in this desire for and pursuit of holiness at the core of one's resulting identity as a child of God.

Calvin's writing on the Christian life is very forthright, showing from Scripture that this is the expected result of grace continuing to work in a person's life. Linked back to his doctrine of election and the work of grace in salvation, without this transforming grace it is possible that a person has received only the first light and ultimately will not turn out to be one of God's elect.

The spirituality that comes from this is very difficult to balance well. It certainly contradicts any idea that God, having accepted us as the sinners we are, allows us to continue in the same state and overlook ongoing sin in our lives. Holiness is not something we wander into or simply aspire to, but something that requires work and dedication and sacrifice in cooperation with God's grace. There is a danger on the other hand that a legalism will come back into the Christian life, that works become part of a sense of duty, and failures lead to guilt and fear. This can be how churches communicate the necessity of holiness, but it is not in line with Calvin's approach.

The growth in holiness is rather a result of grace, a process effected by grace through faith, something we desire as part of our greater desire to glorify and worship God, something that we cannot help working at because of all that God has done in saving us. I find the marriage metaphor helpful in this: that I pursue dedication to my wife in every aspect of my life (not always successfully) as a natural result of the love covenant that we are in.

While human works do not merit or achieve salvation in any of these views, there is an absolute expectation from all of the thinkers that a chief result of salvation is a growth in holiness and in service of others; that no Christian can claim to have been saved by grace through faith unless they demonstrate the ongoing work of the Spirit in their lives. Perhaps this is one aspect that could have come through more in this presentation, particularly on Calvin's thought but also in others: the vital role of the Spirit for every Christian – a challenge for some churches today that have become at times unhelpfully locked into a "Christ alone" rhetoric.

Free Will

This is a bit of an add-on to the main themes of the chapter, but is important in that it relates to the grace/faith discussion as regards the priority of grace and the role of the human being in responding to this grace in faith. It also seems necessary to include this given that our society is absolutely determined that humankind has complete free will, and such a view seems to have permeated the church without much consideration of its validity.

The Reformation background to this theme is not overly complicated. The early church that was working primarily in the Greek language affirmed continuing human free will after the fall, including a will that could respond to God's offer of grace. Things changed in the West in Augustine's later theology that denied any freedom of the will, claiming that it was utterly enslaved by sin until it was liberated by a specific work of grace. Given Augustine's defining position in the history of Western theology, it is unsurprising that this view tended to become the standard, although from the beginnings of the renewal of Christian thought there was a sense that the extreme Augustinian position should be balanced somewhat to allow for some freedom to be retained.

The medieval period continued to incline towards Augustine's teaching, however, with Thomas Aquinas for instance allowing for free choice but not free will (to put it in simple, practical terms: free choice means I get to choose which cereal I eat; the will determines that I must eat). It is only close to the Reformation that we begin to find writers with a much more exalted view of the human will allowing a huge amount of freedom, and one important figure who taught this and was a spark for the Reformation was Desiderius Erasmus.

Erasmus wrote a lengthy treatise on human free will, including considerations of Scripture and of thinkers throughout the history of the church. This work provoked possibly Luther's greatest critique above all the other doctrines and ideas that he disagreed with. In Luther's opinion, expressed in his book *On the Bondage of the Will*, Erasmus had shown contempt for both the Bible and the church in his arguments and had bowed instead to the wisdom of the world. Luther's concentration was on free will and salvation, rather than on any aspect of human society, and it is clear that he believed there was no free will involved in a person's salvation: a point he explicitly made against Erasmus.

Zwingli's focus on the sovereignty of God in all things led him to take a similar position to Luther, while Calvin had an experience very like Luther's in this area, responding in this instance to Pighius, who had argued for human free will. Calvin wrote a book entitled *On the Bondage and Liberation of the Will* in which he takes up the standard position of the church from Augustine, and castigates Pighius for his appalling arrogance in claiming a role for humanity in salvation. In the *Institutes*, when Calvin writes of the will he does allow that society reflects a degree of freedom and goodness in the will in purely earthly terms, but clearly distinguishes between this and the response to God's grace.

It was noticeable when working on the major Protestant reformers for my *Sin, Grace, Free Will* book that each of them explicitly states that they consider humanity to have no free will regarding salvation, and they are vehemently opposed to any voices that would grant any role to the human person. In Protestant churches today I do not see such a view being reflected and, in this area, what is commonly taught now would then have been taught only by some sections of the Catholic Church.

The Catholic Church at the Council of Trent seeks to reflect its developing position over the last few centuries. Trent does state that a person is "not able, by their own free will, without the grace of God, to move themselves into justice in his sight" and condemns anyone who argues "that a person may be able more easily to live justly and to merit eternal life, as if by their own free will without grace, they were able to do both, though hardly indeed and with difficulty". However, free will is not extinguished in the view of the Council of Trent, and there is condemnation for anyone who would teach what might be termed "irresistible grace":

> *If anyone says that a person's free will, moved
> and excited by God, by assenting to God exciting
> and calling it, in no way co-operates towards
> disposing and preparing itself to obtain the grace of
> Justification, that the will cannot refuse its consent
> if it would, but that, as something inanimate, it does
> nothing whatever and is merely passive, let them be
> condemned.*

Shortly after our period, the early decades of the Reformation, the Catholic Church would struggle with this area because of two notable voices, each on one extreme end of the free will spectrum. De Molina, the head of the Jesuit Order, taught very positively on the human will in comparison to most of the work done during the Reformation period; shortly after this, Cornelius Jansen brought a strong Augustinian, negative position back into focus in his work. Both attracted parts of the Catholic Church, and the controversies that resulted between people who remained within that church showed the breadth of thought that it was possible to hold within a Catholic theology.

CONCLUSION

This chapter has attempted to recognize some of the nuances that were present in Reformation discussions concerning the human response to God's grace in salvation and the ongoing effects of that in the Christian life. The concept of faith fascinates me, and it is frustrating to see so much rationality imposed on our understanding of faith – it is interesting that Terry Pratchett, himself an atheist, actually used the concept of faith better in some of his "Discworld" novels than many Christians do when talking about this area.

If we can understand faith better, one result should be a different approach to children in church. Children work much more naturally with faith concepts than adults do; as people grow up they want to understand, to be able to rationalize, rather than just to accept and be absolutely reliant on another. We need to learn again what it is to have faith, and then to find the right approach to building our belief systems, not as final solutions to all theological problems but as investigations into the revelation of our awesome God. Beliefs should primarily enrich our worship and our prayer lives as our faith is expanded by some comprehension of the majesty of God so that it is easier to have faith as I realize how small and weak I am in comparison with my God.

Belief then does not become an end in itself, but a pursuit that naturally follows on from the faith that grace awakens that leads back to greater faith. Likewise, my faith in a God who has saved me and who loves me should compel me to be holy as he is holy, to love my God and my neighbour with every aspect of my being. Not that these "works" become ends in themselves, but they are forms of my worship and, again, as they are done in cooperation with God's grace, they show me God at work in me and through me and my faith again grows.

Some slightly false separations between categories may be apparent in this chapter, but the purpose is to help us think better about aspects of our Christian lives, inspired by some of the relevant writings from the period of the Reformation.

CHAPTER FIVE

PERSECUTION

This chapter differs from previous ones in that it moves on from studying the background and nature of the reforms proposed in the early sixteenth century to consider how they affected persecution. There was no massive reform of the approach to persecution in any Reformation thought but, given that it was a notable feature of that period – particularly in the English context – it seems worthwhile to include this short study of persecution, and especially martyrdom.

An Approaching Challenge?

Persecution comes in many forms, but those faced by the church in Britain in recent centuries have been mild in comparison with those experienced elsewhere in the world and through the history of the church. For much of this time, this was because of the strong influence of the Anglican Church, which meant that persecution was limited to non-conformists and Catholics, although harsh treatment of even these two groups is a distant memory.

In recent years, there have been a number of high-profile cases of Christians who have been singled out in public for issues relating to living out their faith in society, and some have suffered from the scrutiny, from losing jobs, and even from being taken to court and judged. The determination of such people to remain faithful should not be underestimated, but it is difficult to compare them to the experience of the church in China or in parts of the Arab world. Their impact on the church's consciousness arises as much from a comparison with the safe situation of Christians in the West for so long as from the details of the incidents themselves.

It is likely, although not certain, that greater pressure will come upon the church in Britain, but this does depend on the core values that drive its teaching and life. There is some debate about whether the United Kingdom is still a "Christian country"; I would question whether it was *ever* a Christian country. Many of its laws have Christian roots and many of its leaders have had a living faith, but it has never been a theocracy, and the influence of culture and philosophy has been plain not only in society but also in the various expressions of church that have developed. Certain groups have at times challenged the results – John Wesley would be a classic example of someone dissatisfied with the Anglicanism of his time – but the new groups that arose were still products of their surroundings and the values of their time and place rather than "pure" Christianity in a cultural vacuum.

There has been accommodation on the part of both society and the church, with a respect on the one side for the contribution that Christian morality can make and an appreciation on the other of safety and freedom to minister. Things are changing now, as Britain recognizes that in a constitutional monarchy the state has a responsibility to govern for the benefit of all its citizens and with society seeking to build a national identity that allows for the plurality of belief and unbelief that exists.

The result for the church in a loss (though not absence) of influence in politics and society is seen by some as an attack on the church itself, whereas scripturally and historically it would seem that the church is returning to a more expected relationship with the culture, in the world but not of the world. Under Christendom it often seems to have been difficult for the church to fulfil a prophetic role (in the sense of speaking into the current society, rather than predicting the future), since it saw itself as foundational to the beliefs, values, and practices of the culture.

The church in twenty-first-century Britain is now facing decisions about its role in relation to society. One overarching message that seems to be agreed on is that the first duty of Christians is to love God and love neighbour (there's a good basis for this in the Bible!), but there remain questions about what this looks like in practice.

There is a tension, commonly expressed by the phrase "hate the sin, love the sinner", that is difficult to put into practice, with a tendency to go too far one way or the other. Increasingly there seems to be an emphasis on making Christianity approachable for those outside, and engaged with the thought world and media of the time in order to be "relevant". There is merit in these motivations, but one must query the extent to which this might distort the faith that is presented.

Two elements in particular suffer because they do not seem to be relevant. The first is the authority of the Bible, an ancient text that requires committed study and an obedient attitude – neither of which is a popular notion today but both of which are necessary foundations for Christian faith and life. That it is written not only in different languages but also in different cosmological, societal, and ethical situations reinforces a sense of the work needed. The second element is a commitment to holiness and purity that requires the sacrifice of self and a battle against our sinful desires, which again is not a message likely to achieve immediate popularity (even inside the church). The early church regarded a holy life as the central feature of individuals and communities, yet today there seems to be something of an acceptance of our fallibility and a perceived cheapness to the grace we receive from God that require no work on our part to be transformed in denial of our sinful selves.

This relates to another part of the problem: an idea that the church and Christians should be liked and accepted by those around them. This seems to stem from the ministry of Jesus and an understanding that, with crowds following him and the miracles he performed, he was a figure of admiration and love. But this is true only in regard to those who believed in him as far as they were able to understand who he was. It disagrees not only with the attitude of the leaders of the time, but also with Jesus' own summary of his experience: "If the world hates you, keep in mind that it hated me first" (John 15:18). This is because, for those who did not believe, his message challenged their whole understanding of God, faith, and life.

The Christian love of neighbour is not solely about caring for them in the problems of this world. It should certainly manifest itself in this, following the example of Christ, but this cannot be the final end in itself and must be framed in terms of a person's eternal destiny. While the kingdom of heaven has broken into this world through Christ in the power of the Spirit, all the restorative grace that we see in us and through us is as nothing and counts for nothing unless it is tied into the grace of salvation for the age to come.

A Christian love, therefore, that does not at some point include a challenge to make a choice about the work of Christ in overcoming sin and death and judgment can barely be called a love at all. In an attempt not to offend, the role of the church to speak to society of eternal matters seems to have been lost. Yet the gospel message, for all the grace and love it contains, makes sense only in the light of a judgment day when there will be a separation between those who have responded in faith and those who have not. As nice a message as universalism (the salvation of all, regardless of personal faith) may sound, it was not preached by Christ nor is it found in the rest of Scripture.

Not only is this a concern in the message of the church to the world, but it seems to be missing from the faith and life inside churches. There are dangers of what is termed an "over-realized eschatology" (the phrase sounds almost medically dangerous), which means concentrating too much on the kingdom here rather than the kingdom to come. The results of such a view are that a person puts too much emphasis on their identity and life now rather than their eternal identity, and time, energy, and finances are thus spent on things that will pass away rather than things that last. I count myself privileged to be able to spend time occasionally with the monks at Prinknash Abbey near Gloucester because of the challenge they set me in this regard. I am not called to be a monk, but their life speaks to me of a readiness to give up everything I have in this life to serve God wherever I am and whatever I do.

Such an approach to life goes against the mood of the times, which focuses on self-fulfilment here and now rather than on taking up our crosses and being faithful even at the cost of our lives. A devotion to a holy life rather than just "being myself" speaks to the world of the core of the gospel message. For a very long time in Britain, there has been little pressure to make major choices about letting our values stand out from the culture around the church, but this is changing. For our brothers and sisters around the world this has been a common feature of life, and it is often the immigrant churches that are teaching us about the effects our faith should have on our relationship with the world around us and that this can mean antagonism and suffering.

There is also much to learn from the history of the church about persecution and suffering for the faith, and the time of the Reformation provides one window onto this.

READING ABOUT PERSECUTION

In the last section of this chapter, I will provide two paraphrased accounts from near-contemporary sources of Reformation martyrdoms. The Greek word from which we derive the word "martyr" simply means "witness" and this gives an indication of how we might approach such texts well. The stories are often extremely harrowing and therefore praying for peace before we start is important; there can be some gory details that our society would tend to glamorize, and some may need to be aware of this temptation; above all, we read witness statements not simply to be informed but to be challenged about how we live our lives for Christ, and we should be prepared to be changed as a result of what we read.

For me, the martyrs of the faith are important because, however long ago or wherever in the world they lived, they are not only my brothers and sisters but members of the one body of Christ of which I am a part and from which I cannot be separated. The prayer taken from the words of St Patrick puts this beautifully:

I arise today
Through the strength of the love of Cherubim,
In obedience of angels,
In the service of archangels,
In hope of resurrection to meet with reward,
In prayers of patriarchs,
In predictions of prophets,
In preaching of apostles,
In faith of confessors,
In innocence of holy virgins,
In deeds of righteous men.

Each day, in each situation I face, not only is Christ with me by his Spirit but the whole church is with me as I am with them. When I face difficulties, it is a massive support to know that I am not alone but that men and women who have walked faithfully through greater darkness are present with me. When I struggle with temptations, I know that those who have resisted to the point of death are with me and I am challenged to persevere more resolutely (although not always successfully).

This is one of many areas of the faith where the individualism of our times can have a negative impact on the life of the believer, as it obscures the communal identity that the Bible says we have as part of the race of Adam and thus under sin, as part of the children of Abraham as those of faith, and as part of the new covenant body of Christ by the power of the Spirit. When I spend time at Prinknash Abbey, a standard part of the evening meal readings is to have some excerpts from the "Martyrology", a book that describes the life, work, and death of people throughout the history of the church. This is always a poignant time and a worthy reminder of the wider community of which we are part.

Various aspects can come through in an account of a Christian martyr. One important point to bear in mind is that these are not written as neutral, objective records but, as with almost all history, have a purpose that affects the choice, arrangement, and presentation of the material. The author's voice naturally comes through strongly in such a powerfully emotive subject and we should not read blindly as if this were not the case.

One of the works from which our stories come exemplifies this principle in the various prefaces to different editions. John Foxe's *Actes and Monuments of these Latter and Perillous Dayes , Touching Matters of the Church* (more commonly known as the *Book of Martyrs*, a later title) was one of the most-read books in early English Protestantism. Four editions were published during Foxe's lifetime, but some of these had multiple different prologues aimed at guiding groups of readers in how to read the book. The first edition had notable prologues for Catholic, readers claiming that the purpose was to highlight "the pitiful slaughter of your butchery", a rather less humble approach than that proposed above; other prologues were aimed at Protestant readers, in both Latin and English, often highlighting the book as a source for learning about the true Christian faith.[14]

With this warning in mind not to treat them as simple histories and an encouragement to learn more about the faith community of which we are a part, it remains only to highlight some of the common lessons that are taught in the stories of the Christian martyrs. These are unlikely to be a bunch of surprises, but they are worth looking at before we get to some accounts from the Reformation.

---

14   For those interested in more details on this, John King has published a thorough analysis of the Prologue of Foxe's work in *The Huntingdon Library Quarterly*, which is freely available online.

The first aspect highlighted is a desire to be faithful to God despite the natural temptation to spare oneself the suffering that is coming. In many cases, such as that of Thomas Cranmer, weaknesses in the person come through as the story is recounted and this prevents a glorification of the martyr that might stop the reader from being able to identify to some extent with them. This can be seen in more recent cases such as the Chinese Church under Chairman Mao, where we hear about people being gripped by fear and yet willing to undergo suffering. We will look at confidence, but this should not divert our minds from the very real fear of suffering and death. Indeed, we can see this with Christ himself as he faced the prospect of the cross in his prayers in Gethsemane.

In some ways, this faithfulness is an expression of the faith/belief matrix that we have looked at as part of the human response to salvation. Therefore, it has an inherent weakness because it involves a fundamental human element. The second noteworthy aspect relates to our study of grace, since it is a confidence in what God has accomplished on the cross and what God will do in bringing believers into eternal life. Possibly the greatest witness that the martyrs of the church provide is this eternal focus, that whatever things look like in this life there is a greater life that we already participate in.

The earliest and one of the best writers on this was Irenaeus of Lyon, who wrote in the context of persecution and ultimately, we believe, suffered a martyr's death. He taught the doctrine of "recapitulation", which states not that Christ descends to us in our sufferings – although he is present by the Spirit – but a greater truth that we are already in some way present with Christ in his glory. The martyrs approaching their deaths exhibit such confidence in this because they are clearly prepared in their faith and their lives for the resurrection, and find their identity in that life to come rather than here in this life. When we look at all the aspects of our lives – our identity, use of time, use of finances, time spent in prayer or watching TV – what is the balance there between our earthly and eternal identities? Where is our first home?

There is an important dynamic when reading accounts of persecution and martyrdom, when there is a temptation to see a distance between the reader and the subject, which creates feelings of deep sympathy and wonder at what that person is able to undergo. Yet as part of the same body of Christ, as a fellow member of the one church, there should be a greater identification with the martyr as one who is suffering with another part of the body that suffers.[15] If I have faith, it is the same faith (though not perhaps to the same degree: a challenge to grow) that the martyrs had in the same God who calls us all to lay down our lives and follow him. The martyrs are not separate from us in their dedication and faithfulness but examples for us to follow in realizing the implications of our faith for our lives.

As we read an account of martyrdom, we should therefore be led to consider various aspects of our God and faith. Firstly there is God himself, who is worthy of our complete devotion and obedience with all that we have and are, as our creator, as our God, and as our saviour who took on human form and died himself with no need to bring us back into relationship with him. The nature of our God and our position before him are clearly shown in these accounts.

Secondly, we see the effects of sin on the world, both in society and sometimes even in the church. The persecution

---

15   There is an interesting extension of this idea to members of the church whom we see sinning in notable ways in that, as corruption is brought into the body, we are to some degree affected by it ourselves. Pushing this further, this should be a great inspiration for us each to seek to live a holy life, as my sins affect others in the body.

of the faithful results from the developed corruptions of humanity that the litany of sins through history has built up, at times bursting out in massive events including direct targeting of Christians for the faith they hold. Perhaps it is hardest when we see Christians targeting other Christians, a sign that sin works not just in the world but also in the church itself. The ultimate power of sin and death has been broken by the cross and resurrection, but while this world lasts its effects continue and God graciously blesses his people with all they need to be in relationship with him and to receive eternal life when they die. Sometimes God gives little more than this and there is great suffering, during which we must trust his divine perspective on us as individuals and as communities of believers, that things have not run away from his control but that there is wisdom, goodness, and love as he allows these events to take place. As we saw when considering belief, we do not need to (and can never) understand fully, but we can have faith that our God is who he has revealed himself to be: the sovereign creator, redeemer, and judge.

Thirdly, we see the power of faith and the strength of the grace that God gives to his people as they rely completely on him for the truth of a life to come as they face a horrific end to life here on earth. There can be a danger when looking to Christ as the model for humanity that, as the incarnate Son of God, we might think he had an unfair advantage in his faithfulness – this is a very poor view of the incarnation. However, there is no such temptation when looking at men and women of faith who have been willing to lay down their lives in faithfulness to God and confidence in the life to come.

In all of this we should be encouraged by the church of which we are part, that there are and always have been great men and women of faith who show the power and peace that the Spirit can bring into our lives – the same Spirit that lives and works in and through each of us. We should also be challenged to consider how closely our lives and identities are entwined with our ultimate resurrection life with God, and how much the things of this world have a seductive power over us. What are *we* willing to give up for the sake of Christ?

THE ACCOUNTS

Here are just two accounts of martyrdom from the time of the Reformation. The first comes from John Foxe's *Book of Martyrs*, chapter sixteen. One of the most famous and widely read books to come out of this period, it traces the history of martyrdom right back to the earliest martyrs in the first century under the emperor Nero and has become a core part of much Protestant spirituality since it was first published as "A History of the Acts and Monuments of the Church" in 1554.

The account is of the death of Thomas Cranmer, the Archbishop of Canterbury who had worked with Henry VIII in the early years of the independent Church of England and who had been vital to its development as the compiler of the Book of Common Prayer, among other works. After Queen Mary's accession, Cranmer was deposed as archbishop, arrested, and imprisoned for treason. According to Foxe, Cranmer was offered restoration to dignity if he renounced his reforming beliefs, and Cranmer ultimately did sign the paperwork that was brought to him, which affirmed his commitment to the authority of the church and the papacy. His fellow bishops, Latimer and Ridley, maintained a steadfast faith and were burned at the stake with Cranmer present at the death of his friends in 1555.

This passage refers to Cranmer's own death the following year. He is in Oxford, where Latimer and Ridley died, and Queen Mary has ordered his execution despite his affirmation of the Catholic faith. Before he dies, the new Catholic Archbishop of Canterbury, Henry Cole, organizes a public event at which Cranmer can declare his acceptance of Catholicism as a last victory over reforming voices in England.

Here is the text. I suggest you spend a short time in prayer before reading it, as it is somewhat harrowing at times.

> *Thomas Cranmer finally came from the prison of Bocardo to St Mary's Church, it being a foul and rainy day. There was a stage set over against the pulpit, a small height above the ground, where Cranmer stood waiting until Cole prepared himself for his sermon.*
>
> *After he had finished his sermon, Cole called back the people who were ready to depart to prayers. "Brothers", said he, "in case any man should doubt this man's sincere conversion and repentance, you shall hear him speak before you. Therefore I ask you, master Cranmer, to now perform that which you promised not long ago, namely, that you would openly express a true and undoubted profession of your faith in order to take away all suspicion from men, and so that all may understand that you are a Catholic indeed."*
>
> *"I will do it", said the archbishop, "and with a good will." Then having risen up and taken off his cap, he began to speak in this way to the people:*

I desire of you, well-beloved brothers in the Lord, that you will pray to God for me, to forgive me my sins, of which I have committed more than any man, both in number and severity. Among all of these, there is one offence which most of all at this time worries and troubles me, of which you shall hear as I talk in its proper place.

Then, putting his hand into his clothing, he drew out his prayer, which he recited to the people ... Then rising, he said:

Every man, good people, desires at the time of his death to give some good word so that others may remember this before their death, and be better as a result. So I ask God to grant me the grace to speak something at this my departure by which God may be glorified, and you may be edified ...

And now because I have come to the final end of my life, on which hangs all my past life and all my life to come, either to live with my master Christ forever in joy or else to be in pain forever with wicked devils in hell, and I see now before my eyes either heaven ready to receive me or else hell ready to swallow me up; I shall therefore declare to you my very faith that I believe, without any colour or pretence, for now is not the time to pretence, whatever I may have said or written in the past.

First, I believe in God the Father Almighty, Maker of heaven and earth. And I believe every article of the Catholic faith, every word and sentence taught by our Saviour Jesus Christ, his apostles and prophets, in the New and Old Testaments.

And now I come to the great thing which so troubles my conscience, more than anything that I ever did or said throughout my whole life, which is the publication of a writing contrary to the truth, which here and now I renounce and refuse as things that were written with my hand but contrary to the truth that I thought in my heart; written for fear of death and to save my life, if that might be. That is, all bills or papers which I have written or signed with my hand since my dethronement [when Cranmer was dismissed as Archbishop of Canterbury], in which I have written many things that are untrue. And since my hand offended, writing contrary to my heart, my hand shall first be punished for it; for if I come to the fire, it shall be burned first.

As for the Pope, I refuse him as Christ's enemy, and as the Antichrist, with all his false doctrine.

At this point, those standing by were all astonished, marvelled, were amazed, looking at each another, their expectations being so notably deceived by Cranmer. I do not think that there was ever any cruelty more notably or more timely deluded and deceived. They undoubtedly looked for a glorious victory and a perpetual triumph in this man's retraction of his faith. But, as soon as they heard these things, they began to let down their ears, to rage, fret and fume, and so much more because they could not revenge their grief upon him – for they could now no longer threaten or hurt him.

And when he began to speak more of the sacrament and of the papacy, some of them began to cry out, yelp and bawl, and especially Cole cried out upon him, "Stop the heretic's mouth and take him away."

And then Cranmer, being pulled down from the stage, was led to the fire … But when he came to the place where the holy bishops and martyrs of God, Hugh Latimer and Nicholas Ridley, were burnt before him for confessing the truth, kneeling down, he prayed to God; and not taking a long time in his prayers, he took off his garments to his shirt and prepared himself for death.

Then an iron chain was tied about Cranmer; when they perceived him to be more steadfast and that he could not be moved from his punishment, they commanded the fire to be set to him.

And when the wood was kindled and the fire began to burn near him, stretching out his arm, he put his right hand into the flame, which he held so steadfast and immovable (saving that once with the same hand he wiped his face), that all men might see his

hand burned before his body was touched. His body
did so endure the burning of the flame with such
constancy and steadfastness that, standing always
in one place without moving his body, he seemed
to move no more than the stake to which he was
bound. His eyes were lifted up to heaven, and many
times he repeated the words "this unworthy right
hand", so long as his voice would allow him to do so.
And using often the words of Stephen, "Lord Jesus,
receive my spirit", in the greatness of the flame, he
gave up his spirit.

I believe the second text is important both in itself and for the light it sheds on one theme of this book, that the reform movements of the sixteenth century should be viewed as multiple approaches to reform of the one church rather than as a split either into two (Protestant and Catholic – an idea that is difficult to hold, given the divisions in the former group) or into six or however many different strands result, depending on the date one looks at.

As the various reforming groups took different approaches to each of the major areas of faith that we have examined in this book, so there were many groups who faced persecution during the time of the Reformation. The group that suffered most were the Anabaptists, who were subjected to both doctrinal condemnation by all other groups and also political oppression by reformed and Catholic states.

John Foxe's book is a wonderful tool for people wanting to engage with the suffering church through history, and one part of the church that suffered in the sixteenth century. But its dominance has somewhat obscured the fact that it was not only reformed people who were killed for their faith, as representatives of each reforming group – including the Catholic Church – suffered.

While Foxe's is the most notable Protestant martyrology (study of the martyrs), there was a Catholic equivalent published in 1583 that told the stories of Catholic martyrs from 1536 to 1582. It was written by Thomas Bourchier and has a rather long title: *Historia Ecclesiastica de Martyrio Fratrum Ordinis Divi Francisci dictorum de Observantia, qui partim in Anglia sub Henrico octavo Rege, partim in Belgio sub Principe Auriaco, partim et in Hybernia tempore Elizabethæ regnantis Reginæ, idque ab anno 1536 usque ad hunc nostrum præsentem annum 1582, passi sunt.*

14

cum impietate coniunctam, inuehi-
tur. Nihil enim verebatur supplicia,
qui semel constituerat pro nomine
Christi vitam cum morte commu-
tare. Vt enim erat in sacris literis
quammaximè versatus, legerat profecto & menti serio impresserat Ma-
thei illud 10. & Lucæ 12. capitibus.
Matheus quidè vbi sic habet, verba
Christi recitandus. Cùm autem tra-
dent vos, nolite cogitare quomodo
aut quid loquamini. Dabitur enim
vobis in illa hora quid loquamini.
Cótigit hoc in Ecclesia sancti Lau-
rentij Londini, quo etiam in loco
apprehensus est statim & ad carce-
rem abductus, qui portæ noue no-
men habet. Conijciuntur in hunc
malefactores maximi, fures, latro-
nes & similis sortis homines. Adeò
autem locus hic fœtidus est & teter
& vt pœdore & squallore pius pa-
ter extinctus gloriosè migrarit ad

15

Dominũ. Exemplũ profecto Christi
hac in re secutus est vir longè excel-
lentissimus. Videns siquidẽ Christus
Ecclesiã suam militantẽ, multis mi-
serijs fore obnoxiã, ad nostram salu-
tem perficiẽdam in terra cõstitutus,
voluit ipse non solũm molestijs cor-
poris animi quæ angorib' infinitis
agitari, verũ etiam atrocissimũ cru-
cis supplicij gen' subire, vt nobis exemplũ relinqueret. Vnde Apostolus
Petrus primæ suæ epistolæ capite se-
cũdo, Christus inquit passus est pro
nobis, vobis relinquens exemplũ vt
sequamini vestigia eius. Secutus est
certè vestigia eius, dum cum iniquis
optimus ipse computatur & pro eo
squallore carceris extigui se nõ egro
animo acceperit verum ad id, quan-
tumuis etiã per acerbi' supplicium,
paratissimo. Pro eo (inquit Isaias 53.
capite) quod tradidit in morte ani-
mam suã & cum sceleratis reputat',

Image of Bourchier's *Historia Ecclesiastica*, part of the account translated below.

I came across this work while researching for the book and thought that it would be good to include an account of a Catholic martyr to go alongside that of Thomas Cranmer. At this point, trouble struck: while the work was popular at the time with Catholic readers, and has been used as a source for encyclopaedic references to some of the figures contained in its pages, it has not yet been made available in any language other than Latin – indeed, the last edition seems to have been published in 1628. This is a great shame, because the stories that it contains demonstrate a close similarity to the spirituality, faithfulness, and dedication contained in Foxe's book.

Undeterred (well, slightly deterred, if I am honest), I resolved to begin to overcome the distance between the church today and this valuable resource by providing the first translation of one account of a Christian martyr from Bourchier's *Historia Ecclesiastica*.[16] Because of my focus on the medieval period my Latin is quite reasonable and I have done my own work on other books, but for this task I deployed my secret weapon – my mother, Marion Knell, who trained and worked as a Latin and Greek teacher. I owe a great debt of thanks to her for this (as do you, if you appreciate it), particularly as she completed the first translation on her own before we began looking at it together. What merit there is below is thus hers, while I take responsibility for parts where my paraphrase has obscured the intent of the original.

The account is that of Thomas Cortt, who died in prison because of his opposition to Henry VIII. It is a fairly brief text, but I hope it manages to convey well the principles of the martyrs that we have looked at in this chapter.

---

16   You can complete the title for yourself, but I'm afraid a translation of the whole work was a step beyond my commitment to this book.

In this year, 1537, in the same month of July, the actual day being the 27th, there was a certain father called Thomas Cortt, of noble birth, yet more excellently noble himself, who influenced people with his extraordinary ability of speaking. He did not hesitate to incite the implacable anger of the king in suggesting a public meeting despite the danger to his head; while he inveighed with most serious speech against both the indomitable pride and the great savagery of the king.

For he feared nothing, having prayed, at the same time deciding to exchange his life for death for the name of Christ. He was as learned as possible in the sacred writings, reading perfectly, and with a fierce mind stressed Matthew chapter 10 and Luke chapter 12. Indeed it is Matthew who records the words of Christ for us to read in this way: "When, however, they hand you over, do not think how you will speak or what you will say. For you will be given at that time what you should say."

This happened in the holy church of Laurent Londinus [in London] in which place indeed he was arrested and immediately taken to the prison which has the name of "The Gate New" [Newgate]. Assembled in this place are the worst criminals, thieves, robbers and men of similar strength. This place is so foetid and full of terror, shame and squalor that the holy father died and went in glory to God. He followed the excellent example of Christ in this matter, a man most excellent by a long way.

*Christ, having established his church militant on
earth to perfect our salvation, seeing it exposed
to so many miseries, himself wanted not only to
be stirred by troubles of the body and the mind,
but even to submit to the terrible atrocities of the
cross that he might leave us an example. Therefore
the apostle Peter writes in his first epistle, in the
second chapter, "Christ suffered for us leaving an
example that we might follow in his footsteps." He
[Thomas Cortt] followed in Christ's footsteps, while
he himself the best was numbered with transgressors
and experienced that extreme squalor of prison;
indeed he received this to his pure soul that was most
prepared through the prayers of the oppressed. For
him (as it says in Isaiah chapter 53), he handed his
soul in death and was counted with sinners that he
might follow precisely the example of Christ in this
part (following chapter 22 of Luke); while counted
with criminals, he went to death in this prison with
many preceding humiliations.*

*God did not wish the holiness of this man to cease
with his death, nor to be obscured in the shadows
of prison, which God showed with a holy sign – by
far the most holy – when he filled the whole prison
with a huge light, all those who were present seeing
and wondering at this new and magnificent event.
So greatly indeed did this trouble the mind of the
king that he said to himself that Cortt was the
most outstanding among the best of men. He –
the king – ordered those who wanted the body to
take it to the tomb of the king himself. And so the*

*body was committed in the cemetery of the most
beautiful tomb, near the gate of the greater church,
superimposed generously with inscriptions on stone
which last to this day. In this place is the inscription:*

You who pass by, a traveller in Christ's service,
in your prayers you will become as it were a
memory of me.

*This stone is placed with one expensive inscription
at the command of the pious lady Margaret Herbert,
wife of a certain craftsman who made this with the
texture of gloves.*

CONCLUSION

There are many groups praying for the persecuted church, and
this is right and proper, as our brothers and sisters around the
world suffer for their faith in ways that we are not yet called to.
I hope that those brothers and sisters are also praying for us,
as the lives that they live and the faith that they realize through
suffering, the eternal life that they expect and too quickly
attain, challenge me to consider how much of my life, my time,
my energies, and my finances are spent in dedication to God in
some form and on things that have eternal value.

I sometimes look at churches' and people's long-term plans
and strategies and wonder whether, if Christ were to come
again next week, there would be a sense of disappointment
that there wasn't time for this event or that conversation. With
the comparative safety of this world, long life expectancy, and
huge opportunities to live, to explore, and to love, the return of

Christ and the judgment that will follow seem to be rather lost in church teaching and in people's expectations.

It is great that we have these witnesses from the past, as well as the present day, who should call us to consider our lives and our priorities, to lift our lives up from what are often comparatively minor, first-world problems and recognize that all we have and are comes from God, and that being home with him in eternal life should be our prime vision and hope.

CHAPTER SIX

SUMMING UP

This study has been all too brief, particularly in the space it has been possible to devote to the Reformation (or reformations) in particular. But I hope that, for many readers, it will be the first stage in rediscovering this crucial time in the history of the church, while it should help others to be aware of what was happening at that time, what some of the key figures believed, and from what basis they developed their teachings.

The first important point is to see that the sixteenth century was not about one Catholic Church and one Protestant Church, that there was no single Reformation, and nor was what happened a division, as it sometimes appears. If there is one body of Christ, there is only one church, and in each of the groups we have looked at there were members who believed in the Lord Jesus Christ and who lived with the Spirit in expectation of eternal life with God. It was recognized, most explicitly by Luther and Calvin, that while there were disputes with institutions, teachings, and members of other groups, there were also fellow Christians present under other labels. We must be careful not to cut Christ's body into pieces, especially when dealing with movements such as those that constituted the Reformation.

Secondly, we need to recognize the different strands of thought that were present through the period known as *the* Reformation. In many areas, Luther had more in common with the Catholic Church of his time than with someone like Müntzer, who had a large number of protesting followers. Reform was necessary, but the precise areas of teaching and life that needed reform, the scriptural, theological, and philosophical tools that would be used to accomplish this, and the degree and result of the reforms were different in every case – and the generic approaches presented in this book could be subdivided many times by smaller movements or quieter voices from the period. Various reformations occurred, some of which lasted, some of which faded away, and some of which were transformed by later generations into churches that bear little resemblance to the originators of reform.

The next point to highlight is that, in the vast majority of cases, these were "reformers" of the church, not people or movements that wanted to start again from scratch and take everything back to just the Bible, or even just to Augustine. There were redefinitions of the church by some groups to remove it from its political, papal, scholastic, and even monastic manifestations, but there was still a sense of being part of one church dating back through history, which God had guided and yet which had fallen into errors in its teaching and practice. As I have tried to show, the reformers were generally looking back to find good understandings of the Christian faith and life so as to call the church back to what it should have been and what at times it had been.

Finally, given that modern Protestant movements trace their origins back to Reformation times and to these thinkers, it is surprising how much of their thought is ignored by the churches today, some of which bear their names. If the 500th anniversary had focused more on actually going back to the writings of the reformers, there would have been a recognition of this gap and even, possibly, a fresh lens through which we could look at the churches of today: what would Luther, Zwingli, or Calvin have said about the teaching and actions of people in Protestant churches today? Would they recognize something that derived from their work? Even if they could find some traces, I'm afraid they would find far more that they would consider to be in need of reform.